The Child Support Enforcement (CSE) Program is a Federal/state/local partnership to collect child support: We want to send the strongest possible message that parents cannot walk away from their children. Our goals are to ensure that children have the financial support of both their parents, to foster responsible behavior towards children, to emphasize that children need to have both parents involved in their lives, and to reduce welfare costs.

The Federal CSE Program was established in 1975 as Title IV-D of the Social Security Act. It functions in all states and territories, through the state/county Social Services Department, Attorney General's Office, or Department of Revenue. Most states work with prosecuting attorneys, other law enforcement agencies, and officials of family or domestic relations courts to carry out the program at the local level. Native American Tribes, too, can operate child support programs in the context of their cultures and traditions with Federal funding.

State Child Support Programs locate noncustodial parents, establish paternity, establish and enforce support orders, modify orders when appropriate, and collect and distribute child support payments. While programs vary from state to state, their services are available to all parents who need them.

The Federal Office of Child Support Enforcement (OCSE) is part of the U.S. Department of Health and Human Services. It helps states develop, manage, and operate their programs effectively and according to Federal law. OCSE pays the major share of state program operating costs, provides location services, policy guidance and technical help to enforcement agencies, conducts audits and educational programs, supports research, and shares ideas for program improvement.

We believe that child support enforcement provides hope as well as support to America's children. We dedicate this Handbook to the millions of parents who put their children first by responsibly providing for their emotional and financial support.

OFFICE OF CHILD SUPPORT ENFORCEMENT
Giving Hope and Support to America's Children

HANDBOOK ON CHILD SUPPORT ENFORCEMENT

U.S. Department of Health and Human Services
Administration for Children and Families
Office of Child Support Enforcement
Washington, D.C. 20447

Updated 2005 and 2008

Foreword

This Handbook on Child Support Enforcement is a guide to help you get the child support payments your children need and deserve. Although it is written for people who are working through Child Support Enforcement (CSE) offices, it will also be useful to parents who are working with private attorneys.

To ensure that children have *parentage* established and to establish fair child support payments, state CSE programs provide:

- Voluntary in-hospital paternity acknowledgement
- *Genetic testing* at the request of either party in disputed paternity cases
- Child support *guidelines* for determining child support orders established in each state
- Review of child support orders at least every three years at the request of either parent

Tools that are available to collect child support include:

- *Income withholding*
- Revocation of drivers, professional, recreational and occupational licenses of parents who are not current in their child support payments
- Seizure of assets, including financial accounts
- Liens on property
- Denial of passports
- Federal and state tax refund offset

To ensure that state and local child support offices have access to information, the Federal government operates the Federal Parent Locator Service (FPLS), which includes the *Federal Case Registry (FCR)* and the *National Directory of New Hires (NDNH)*. The FPLS has access to information from state and Federal government agencies. The FCR maintains caseload information from all states and territories. The Administration for Children and Families (ACF) Office of Child Support Enforcement (OCSE) has a website for people who have access to the Internet. The site provides current information about the CSE program, policy matters, state and Federal office addresses, links to state websites, a frequently asked questions section, and links to related agencies. The web address is: http://www.acf.hhs.gov/programs/cse.

* Words in *italics* are defined in the Glossary.

TABLE OF CONTENTS

I. INTRODUCTION

Are you a parent – divorced, separated or never married--with children to support?

Are you a *noncustodial* parent with questions about your rights and responsibilities?

Do you need to locate a parent? …establish paternity? …get a child support order?

Do you need help to collect child support?

Are you pregnant, or the parent of a child, and thinking about marriage?

In this <u>Handbook,</u> you will find the basic steps to follow to establish paternity, to obtain a support order, and to collect the support due, whether you are working with your state, local, or tribal *Child Support Enforcement* (CSE) program or your own attorney. There is information for noncustodial parents about providing financial and emotional support to your children, about keeping in touch with them, and keeping support orders fair. Although the function of the CSE program is to collect and distribute child support payments, throughout the <u>Handbook</u> we hope to give the message that children fare best when both parents play an active, supportive role in their lives.

The CSE Program is run by the states, usually in the Human Services Departments, Attorney Generals' Offices, or Departments of Revenue. Several Native American tribes have established CSE programs as well. Child support enforcement is handled according to state or tribal laws and practices. The states and tribes determine the forum under which child support activities take place. In this <u>Handbook,</u> we will use the term "*tribunal*" to refer to the office (court, judicial, or administrative) with authority to make legally binding decisions.

The <u>Handbook</u> is organized so that you can refer directly to the sections you need. Your state's CSE program is available to help:

- Find a noncustodial parent: **Location**

- Establish legal fatherhood for children: **Paternity**

- Establish and maintain a fair, financial and medical support order: **Obligation**

- Enforce support orders: **Enforcement**

- Distribute the money that is collected: **Distribution**

- With Interstate, Tribal, and International Enforcement: **Working across Borders**

We have added sections to the <u>Handbook</u> to address:

- The Child Support Program and Healthy Marriage: **Healthy Marriage Initiative**

- Rights and responsibilities of the noncustodial parent: **Noncustodial Parents**

- Child Support Program progress: **Lessons Learned**

* Words in *italics* are defined in the Glossary.

The more you take an active role in learning about the CSE program, and in getting information to your caseworker, the more success you will have in obtaining regular and full child support payments for your children.

This <u>Handbook</u> gives basic information. To learn more about how the program will work for you, or to apply for child support services, call your local CSE office. Check the county listings in your telephone book to get the telephone number, or call or write the state CSE agency listed at the back of this <u>Handbook</u>. (CSE agency toll-free numbers, when available, are listed too.)

If you have access to the internet, there is a listing of CSE agencies at: http://ocse.acf.hhs.gov/int/directories/index.cfm?fuseaction=main.extivdlist

State CSE websites often give the addresses and telephone numbers for local offices: http://www.acf.hhs.gov/programs/cse/extinf.html

There is a listing of tribal CSE agencies at: http://ocse.acf.hhs.gov/int/directories/index.cfm?fuseaction=main.tribalivd

Un listado de las agencias de CSE en español se puede encontrar en: http://ocse.acf.hhs.gov/int/directories/index.cfm?fuseaction=main.extEspanolIVd

La información de la ayuda del niño en español está disponible en: http://www.acf.hhs.gov/programs/cse/fct/childspan.pdf http://www.acf.hhs.gov/programs/cse/spanish/booklet.pdf

***

Property settlement, visitation and custody are not, by themselves, child support enforcement issues and the CSE Program generally cannot establish or enforce orders relating to them. However, each state receives grant money from the Federal Office of Child Support (OCSE) to develop model programs to ensure that children have access to both their parents. Your state CSE agency can tell you about the program in your state, and if there are other resources through the courts or other systems set up by the state.

***

If unmarried parents have considered getting married, but need advice, there may be help available though community- or faith-based organizations that teach healthy marriage and parenting skills. These organizations can help couples make good decisions about getting married and about sustaining healthy relationships. There is solid evidence that children whose parents can develop a healthy marriage have greater financial and emotional security. Learning parenting skills (communication, responsibility, child development, etc.), even if the parents decide not to marry, will help them to provide their children with support and stability. The CSE agency may be able to guide parents to the resources available in their states.

Who can get help?

Any parent or person with custody of a child who needs help to establish a child support or medical support order or to collect support payments can apply for child support enforcement services. People who have received assistance under the *Temporary Assistance for Needy Families (TANF), Medicaid,* and *Federally assisted Foster Care* programs are automatically referred for child support enforcement services.

Either parent can get help to have a child support order reviewed at least every three years, or whenever there is a substantial change of circumstances, to ensure that the order remains fair.

An unmarried father can apply for services to establish paternity -- a legal relationship with his child.

A *noncustodial parent* whose case is not in the CSE Program can apply for services and make payments through the Program. Doing so ensures that there is a record of payments made.

Location services are available for noncustodial parents whose children have been hidden from them in violation of a custody or visitation order.

Although the majority of custodial parents are mothers, keep in mind that either the mother or father may have primary custody of the child.

Where do I apply for help in obtaining child support?

You can apply through the state or local child support enforcement (CSE) office. Usually, applying to your local CSE agency is most effective; however, you have the right to apply to another tribunal if that will result in more efficient service. The telephone numbers for state CSE Agencies can be found in telephone directories, usually under the state/county social services agency, at the end of this Handbook, or on the state's child support website. These sites are linked at: http://www.acf.hhs.gov/programs/cse/extinf.html

What does the child support enforcement agency need to know?

No matter where you start -- establishing paternity, finding a noncustodial parent, establishing or enforcing a support order -- the CSE office must have enough information to work on your case effectively. All information you provide will be treated in confidence. The more details you provide, the easier it will be to process your case and to collect child support payments for your children.

What documents do I need to bring to the enforcement agency?

Bring as much as you can of the following information and documents. This will help the CSE office to locate the parent, establish paternity, and establish and/or enforce your child support order.

• Information about the noncustodial parent

> • name, address and Social Security number
> • name and address of current or recent employer
> • names of friends and relatives, names of organizations to which he or she might belong
> • information about his or her income and assets -- pay slips, tax returns, bank accounts, investments or property holdings
> • physical description, or photograph, if possible

• birth certificates of children

• if paternity is an issue, written statements (letters or notes) in which the alleged father has said or implied that he is the father of the child

• your child support order, divorce decree, or separation agreement if you have one

• records of any child support received in the past

• information about your income and assets

• information about expenses, such as your child's health care, daycare, or special needs

You play a big role in getting the child support your children deserve.

Is there an application fee?

People receiving assistance under Medicaid, Foster Care, or cash assistance programs do not have to pay for CSE services. For all others, a fee of up to $25 is charged, although some states absorb all or part of the fee or collect payment from the noncustodial parent.

Are there any other costs?

Because child support agencies may recover all or part of the actual costs of their services from people who are not in a public assistance program, there may be other costs to parents. These can include the cost of legal work done by agency attorneys, costs of establishing paternity, and costs of locating a noncustodial parent. The costs may be deducted from the child support payment before it is sent to you or may be collected from the noncustodial parent. Not all states recover the costs of their services. Your local CSE office can tell you about the practices in your state.

In addition, there is a $25 annual fee for those individuals who do not receive public assistance after the State has collected and disbursed $500 on their behalf in a given year. In some States, this fee is charged to the noncustodial parent, in others it is charged to the custodial parent. States also have the option to pay the fee themselves or take it out of the child support collection. Your local CSE office can tell you about the practices in your state.

My state recovers costs from the custodial parent. How will I know how much will be deducted from my support checks?

Your caseworker should be able to estimate the costs involved in your case, and give you an idea of how much they will deduct from each check before sending it to you.

Will there be an extra cost if the enforcement agency is dealing with the enforcement agency in another state?

There may be extra costs if more than one tribunal is handling your case. Ask your caseworker to estimate these costs, if any.

Will the enforcement agency keep track of my child support payments to make sure they keep coming? I am not in a cash assistance program.

CSE offices are required to monitor payments to make sure they are made regularly and fully. But you should inform the agency if payments are late, in the wrong amount, or if you receive payments directly. When you monitor your case, you can keep the CSE office informed so that it can act quickly if needed.

The noncustodial parent lives across the state. I cannot afford to take the time off from work or to travel there for a child support hearing. How can I get enforcement of my child support?

Most local CSE offices handle enforcement in different jurisdictions in the same state without your having to travel outside your own jurisdiction. Ask your local CSE office for details about how enforcement would work in your case.

I am applying for TANF. Do I have to provide information about the father?

To be eligible for assistance programs, you must provide information to help to identify the father and collect child support from him. Any child support collected will be used to help support your children -- going either directly to you or to repay the state for your assistance grant. Your state CSE agency will explain how the child support will be used.

I don't have any way to support my baby without help, but her father is dangerous. I'm afraid to tell the caseworker who he is.

If you think that you or the baby would not be safe if you try to establish paternity or collect child support, and you need to be in a cash assistance program, you can talk with your caseworker about showing *good cause* for not naming the father. There are safeguards in place to protect you, such as a *family violence indicator* that can be placed in your records so that your personal information is not released to anyone who is not authorized to view it.

My children and I need money now. The noncustodial parent left us ten years ago. Can the CSE office still take my case?

If you apply for services, the CSE office will try to find the noncustodial parent to establish or enforce a child support obligation. Be sure to give your caseworker all the information you have that might help find the parent.

II. FINDING THE NONCUSTODIAL PARENT: LOCATION

In most cases, to establish the paternity of a child, to obtain an order for support, and to enforce that order, the Child Support Enforcement (CSE) agency must know where the other parent lives or works. When one person makes a legal claim against another, the *defendant* must be given notice of the legal action taken and the steps necessary to protect his or her rights. To notify the noncustodial parent in advance under the state's service of process requirements – for example, by certified mail or personal service – child support enforcement officials need a correct address. If you do not have the address, the CSE office can try to find it. The most important information that you can provide is the noncustodial parent's Social Security number and any employer that you know about.

State/tribal CSE agencies, with due process and security safeguards, have access to information from the following:

- State and local government:

  vital statistics
  state tax files
  real and titled personal property records
  occupational and professional licenses and business information
  employment security agency
  public assistance agency
  motor vehicle department
  law enforcement departments

- Records of private entities like public utilities and cable television companies (such as names and addresses of individuals and their employers as they appear in customer records)

- Credit bureaus

- Information held by financial institutions, including asset and liability data.

- The *State Directory of New Hires,* to which employers must report new employees

- The *Federal Parent Locator Service (FPLS)*

The FPLS, which includes the *Federal Case Registry (FCR)* and *the National Directory of New Hires (NDNH)*, has access to information from:

- The Internal Revenue Service (IRS), the Department of Defense, the National Personnel Records Center, including quarterly wage data for Federal employees, the Social Security Administration, and the Department of Veterans Affairs

- *State Directories of New Hires* (SDNH)

- *State Workforce Agencies (SWAs)*

The FCR includes all *IV-D child support* cases from the 54 states and territories and non-IV-D support orders established after October 1998. The NDNH contains new hire records, quarterly wage records for almost all employed people, and unemployment insurance claims.

If you have access to the internet, there is information about the FPLS at: http://www.acf.hhs.gov/programs/cse/newhire

I think the noncustodial parent is still in the area. What information will the enforcement office need to find him?

Most important are the Social Security number and any recent employer's name and address. Also helpful are the names, addresses and phone numbers of relatives, friends, or former employers who might know where he/she works or lives. Unions and local organizations, including professional organizations, might also have information.

What if I don't have the Social Security Number?

Social Security numbers are now required on applications (not the licenses themselves) for professional licenses, drivers' licenses, occupational and recreational licenses, and marriage licenses; on divorce records, support orders, and paternity determinations or acknowledgements; and on death records.

If none of these is available, or the Social Security number was not yet required when the document was issued, the CSE office can *subpoena* information about bank accounts, insurance policies, credit cards, pay slips, or income tax returns. If you and the other parent filed a joint Federal income tax return in the last three years, the CSE office can get the Social Security number from the IRS.

Your caseworker may be able to get the Social Security number with at least three of the following pieces of information: the parent's name, place of birth, date of birth, his/her father's name, and his/her mother's maiden name.

What if the noncustodial parent cannot be found locally?

Your CSE office will ask the *State Parent Locator Service* (SPLS) to do a search. Using the Social Security number, the SPLS will check the records of state agencies such as the motor vehicle department, SWAs, state revenue department, law enforcement agencies, and correctional facilities. If the SPLS finds that the parent has moved to another state, it can ask the other state to search, and send a request to the Federal Parent Locator Service (FPLS).

Can my lawyer or I ask the FPLS to find an address for the other parent?

Not directly. However, you or your attorney can submit a request to use the FPLS through the local or state CSE agency.

If I hire a private collection service, can the state CSE agency provide location and income information?

Yes. The private service must provide a guarantee in writing that the information is to be carefully safeguarded and only used for child support purposes, and it must have an agreement that meets state requirements for acting as an *"agent of the child."*

Can state and Federal location efforts be made at the same time?

Yes. For instance, a search can be initiated by the state to another *jurisdiction* and to the FPLS at the same time. The FPLS matches child support case data with data in the FCR and with the employment data in the NDNH and has access to information from other Federal agencies. Locate information is returned to the state(s) for processing.

Can enforcement agencies use the Federal income tax return to find out where the noncustodial parent lives and what he or she earns?

Yes. Under certain conditions, the IRS, working through the Federal Office of Child Support Enforcement (OCSE), may disclose to the child support office information that income providers submit on IRS Form 1099. This information is a valuable tool to help find a noncustodial parent and determine his or her financial assets. The information may only be used for the purpose of enforcing child support payments.

Information available through Form 1099 includes both earned and unearned income, including wages, earnings on stocks and bonds, interest from bank accounts, unemployment compensation, capital gains, royalties and prizes, and employer and financial institution addresses. Even very small businesses submit 1099 asset information to the IRS, so this can be a good source of information. Any information obtained from the IRS must be verified through a second source, such as an employer or bank, before the CSE agency can use it.

What will happen when the caseworker has the current address of the noncustodial parent?

The worker will verify the home and work addresses, and take the next appropriate action on the case, which may include asking the noncustodial parent to come to the CSE office for an interview, or notifying him/her that legal action may be taken.

The father of my child is in the military, but I don't know where he is stationed. Can the enforcement agency find him?

Yes. The FPLS can provide the current duty station of a parent who is in any of the uniformed services.

If the CSE office can't find the noncustodial parent, does that mean I can't get cash assistance?

No. You can get assistance from the TANF program if you are trying to help find the noncustodial parent. Your state or local CSE agency will tell you what information they will need you to provide in order to get assistance.

III. ESTABLISHING FATHERHOOD: PATERNITY

A father can acknowledge paternity by signing a written admission or *voluntary acknowledgement* of paternity. All states have programs under which birthing hospitals give unmarried parents of a newborn the opportunity to acknowledge the father's paternity of the child. States must also help parents acknowledge paternity up until the child's eighteenth birthday through vital records offices or other offices designated by the state.

Paternity can also be established at a court or administrative hearing or by *default* if the man was served notice of a paternity hearing but did not appear. Parents are not required to apply for child support enforcement services when acknowledging paternity. An acknowledgment of paternity becomes a *finding* of paternity unless the man who signed the acknowledgment denies that he is the father within 60 days. Generally, this finding may be challenged only on the basis of fraud, duress, or material mistake of fact.

If it becomes necessary to seek child support, a finding of paternity creates the basis for the obligation to provide support. A support order cannot be established for a child who is born to unmarried parents until paternity has been established.

It is important to establish paternity as early as possible. While Child Support Enforcement (CSE) offices must try to establish paternity for any child up to the child's 18th birthday, it is best to do it as soon after the child's birth as possible. If a man is not certain that he is the father, the CSE agency can arrange for *genetic testing.* These tests are simple to take and highly accurate.

Even if the parents plan to marry after their baby is born, establishing paternity helps to protect the relationship between the child and the father from the very start.

What are the benefits of establishing paternity?

In addition to providing a basis for child support, paternity establishment can provide basic emotional, social, and economic ties between a father and his child. There are strong indications that children whose fathers take active roles in their upbringing lead more successful lives.

Once paternity is established legally, a child gains legal rights and privileges. Among these may be rights to inheritance, rights to the father's medical and life insurance benefits, and rights to social security and possibly veterans' benefits. The child also has a chance to develop a relationship with the father, and to develop a sense of identity and connection to the "other half" of his or her family. It can be important for the health of the child for doctors to have knowledge of the father's medical history.

What will the CSE agency need to know to try to establish paternity?

The caseworker needs as much information as you can provide about the alleged father and the facts about your relationship with him, your pregnancy, and the birth of your child. Some of these questions may be personal, but states must keep the information that you give confidential.

The caseworker will also want to know whether he ever provided any financial support, or in any other way acknowledged – through letters or gifts – that that the child was his. A picture of the alleged father with the child is helpful, as well as any information from others who could confirm your relationship with him.

What if he denies he is the father, or says he's not sure?

Paternity can be determined by administrative procedures which take into account highly accurate tests conducted on blood or tissue samples of the man, mother and child. Genetic test results indicate a *probability of paternity* and can establish a legal *presumption of paternity.* These tests can exclude a man who is not the biological father and can also show the likelihood of paternity if he is not excluded. Each party in a contested paternity case must submit to genetic tests at the request of either party or the CSE agency.

Because genetic testing is so accurate now, states are struggling with the question of what to do if paternity was established by acknowledgement or because the child was born during a marriage, but later testing proves that the man is not the biological father. Some states have procedures for *disestablishing* paternity. Often, though, when a father/child relationship has been established, states are reluctant to break that bond. State laws and practices determine whether or not paternity can be disestablished.

If genetic tests are necessary, who pays for them?

If the state orders the tests, the state must pay the cost of the testing. If the father is identified by the tests, some states will charge him for their costs.

If a party disputes the original test result, he or she can pay for a second genetic test and the state must then obtain additional testing.

What happens if I am not sure who the father is?

If the father could be one of several men, each may be required to take a genetic test. These tests are very accurate, and it is almost always possible to determine who fathered a baby and to rule out anyone who did not.

My boyfriend is on a military base abroad and I am about to have his baby. How can I establish paternity and get an order for support?

You can apply for child support enforcement services at your local CSE office. If he is willing to sign documents to acknowledge paternity and agree to support, then enforcement can proceed by an income withholding order. If the man is on a naval ship or lives on a military base abroad and will not acknowledge paternity, it may be necessary to wait until he returns to the United States for genetic testing to be done.

The father of my child said I would never get a paternity judgment on him because he'd just leave the state. What happens in this case?

If the accused father fails to respond to a formal *complaint* properly served upon him, a *default judgment* may be entered in court. The default judgment establishes paternity. At the same time, a court order for support may be issued. If the parent has disappeared, state and Federal Parent Locator Services can be called on to help find him. States must give *full faith and credit* to paternity determinations made by other states in accordance with their laws and regulations.

My boyfriend and I are still in high school, and our baby is 6 months old. Why should legal paternity be established if the father has no money to support the child?

When the father gets older and starts working, he will be able to support the child. Having paternity established legally, even if the order for support is minimal or delayed, means collecting child support will be easier later. Aside from establishing a financial commitment from the father, establishing paternity fosters a personal relationship between the father and child.

Some states have laws enforcing child support obligations with respect to minor parents. If a custodial parent is receiving TANF assistance, the parents of the noncustodial minor parent may be responsible for paying child support. Check with your CSE agency to see if your state enforces "grandparent liability."

My baby's father lives out of state. Can I still have paternity established?

Yes, you can. For example, if the baby was conceived in your state, if the father used to live there, or there is another basis for exercising personal jurisdiction, your state can claim "*long arm*" jurisdiction over him, and require that he appear for paternity establishment. If your state cannot claim jurisdiction, the CSE agency can petition the state where he lives to establish paternity. Your caseworker will be able to tell you what needs to be done in your case.

What happens after paternity is established?

If it becomes necessary to establish a child support order, a CSE caseworker may discuss the child's financial and medical needs with the father and what he is required to pay for child support according to the state child support guidelines. If a court issues a child support order later, it may also include the exact terms of custody, visitation, and other parental rights.

I don't want my daughter's father in our lives. I'd rather work two jobs and support my child myself than have him establish paternity. As long as I don't receive public assistance, why does establishing paternity matter?

There are few situations when it is not in children's best interest to have paternity established. Knowing their father and having his emotional and financial support is very important to children. In the future, information may be necessary for medical reasons, and paternity establishment may make obtaining appropriate medical attention easier. Also, remember, the child's father has the right to request genetic testing to prove that he is the father and he can then establish the legal right to a relationship with his child.

My child's father wants to declare paternity. Is there an easy way for him to do this?

All states offer parents the opportunity to voluntarily acknowledge a child's paternity until the child reaches the age of 18. Forms are available at the hospital or from the state vital records agency. More information is available from the CSE agency.

IV. ESTABLISHING THE SUPPORT ORDER: OBLIGATION

If child support enforcement becomes an issue, it is necessary to have a legal order for child support spelling out the amount of the *obligation* and how it is to be paid. Establishing a support order depends on how much success you and your caseworker or lawyer have in several critical areas, such as locating the noncustodial parent, if necessary; identifying what he or she should pay; and determining the financial needs of the child.

All states have child support *guidelines* (a calculation of how much a parent should contribute to the child's financial support) that must be used to establish support orders unless it is shown, in writing, that doing so is not in the best interest of the child. Most state guidelines consider the needs of the child, other dependents, and the ability of the parents to pay. States must use the guidelines unless they can be shown to be inappropriate in a particular case.

Current law requires every *IV-D child support* order to include a provision for health care coverage, and the Child Support Enforcement (CSE) agency is required to pursue private health care coverage when such coverage is available through a noncustodial parent's employer. Medical support can take several forms. The noncustodial parent may be ordered to:

- provide health insurance if available through his/her employer,

- pay for health insurance (health care coverage) premiums or reimbursement to the custodial parent for all or a portion of the costs of health insurance obtained by the custodial parent, and/or

- pay additional amounts to cover a portion of ongoing medical bills or as reimbursement for uninsured medical costs.

States today can have arrangements for establishing the support order by an *administrative procedure* or other expedited legal procedure. The hearing may be conducted by a master or a referee of the court, or by an administrative hearings officer. An order approved by this kind of procedure, whether contested or made by agreement between the parties, must be based on the appropriate child support guidelines for setting a child support order and generally has the same effect as one established in court. It is legally binding on the parties concerned.

If an agreement for support is made between the parents, it should provide for the child's present and future well-being. It may be useful to discuss these issues together if you can, or with a mediator or family counselor. You may call your CSE office or visit the state's website to find out about your state's child support guidelines: http://www.acf.hhs.gov/programs/extinf.html

What is the most important action that a custodial or non-custodial parent can take to ensure that the order amount is fair?

The most important action is to appear at the support order hearing with the documents requested in the notification of the hearing. When both parents appear and bring the necessary documents, the tribunal making the determination will be able to make a fully informed and fair decision.

How does the caseworker find out about the other parent's income or assets?

The caseworker will make every possible effort to identify the parent's employment, property owned, and any other sources of income or assets. This information must be verified before the support order is final. Under certain situations, the Internal Revenue Service may provide financial information about the parent's earned and unearned income, such as interest payments and unemployment compensation. Employers are now required to report hiring people to the state, and the state then provides the information to the *National Directory of New Hires (NDNH)*, which is a part of the *Federal Parent Locator Service (FPLS)*. The FPLS can provide income information from the NDNH and from states' quarterly wage records. The state CSE agency now has access to financial institution data, such as bank accounts and credit bureau data, which may provide information about employers and/or assets.

I'm sure the other parent is willing to pay support. Can we make an agreement between ourselves and present it to the court?

Laws vary from state to state, but parents who can work out a fair support agreement between themselves can avoid the discord that may occur with contested support hearings. You can get help from a lawyer, mediator or family counselor to present your proposal to the court or administrative hearing officer. The court's sole interest in your agreement is to see that it is fair to all parties, that the welfare of the children is protected, and that the agreement reflects the guidelines.

Are the earnings of both parents considered in setting support awards?

Some states base their guidelines on both parents' incomes (an income-share model), some only on the income of the noncustodial parent (a percentage model). In the models based only on the noncustodial parent income, it is presumed that the custodial parent is contributing towards the child(ren)'s needs by providing care, food, clothing, and shelter.

My wife and I are working out a joint custody agreement. How would the court decide the amount of child support for each of us?

That depends a lot on the terms of your custody agreement and on your state's child support guidelines: Some states have guideline formulas that take joint custody into account. The same factors would apply: state guidelines, each parent's ability to pay, and the needs of the child.

My husband's income is enough to support the children and me without a drop in our standard of living after the divorce. Do the courts consider this?

These decisions, again, are based on the state's guidelines. However, when one or both parents have high income, the tribunal may decide that strict application of the guidelines is not in the best interest of the children. Such a decision may result in a higher and more appropriate support amount than the amount recommended by the guidelines.

I have custody and I just heard that my son's mother has had three promotions in the last four years but the child support is still like it was six years ago. Is there some way to find out when she has a raise?

CSE offices will review child support orders at least every three years, or if there is a significant change of circumstances, if either parent requests such a review. Some states have a procedure for an automatic update. Ask your caseworker for information about reviewing and, if appropriate, modifying your child support order. As part of the review, the caseworker will verify the current income of the noncustodial parent. States can adjust child support orders according to child support guidelines, a cost of living adjustment, or automated methods determined by the state.

What can I do to get my support increased if it is too low?

Check with your CSE office to see if your support order should be modified. The agency will consider the income and assets of the *noncustodial parent;* and, in many states, your financial situation; and any special needs of the child. If your support amount is found to be low based on the current financial situation, the agency can seek a legal modification.

My ex-husband has remarried and has another family to support. How will this affect the support that my children are due?

Even though the noncustodial parent has a second family, this does not eliminate responsibility to the first family. In some states, the judge may grant the noncustodial parent a decrease in the obligation based on application of the child support guidelines. You must be notified beforehand and given an opportunity to contest the proposed change. Other factors that could lower the support order include increases in your earnings, or poor health or decreased earning ability of the noncustodial parent. If your child leaves school and becomes employed, that can reduce, or stop, child support payments, too.

My children's father is divorcing again and will have another child support order. He lives in another state and I'm afraid that this other order will be enforced before mine.

State guidelines may indicate how child support is to be shared when there is more than one support order. If his income will not provide for both orders, the amount of support for your children may be reduced, but you will receive a share of the support collected. For orders enforced by income withholding, states must have a formula for sharing the available income among the support orders. Each family must receive a portion of the available money, and current support has priority over arrearages. Depending on your state child support guidelines, it is also possible that the second support order may be grounds for his requesting a modification of your order. Ask your caseworker for more information.

I am the custodial parent. I can't get health insurance with my job but my ex-wife gets good benefits where she works. Can she be required to put the children on her insurance?

Yes. The CSE agency must petition the court to include *medical support* in any order for child support when employment related or other group health insurance is available to the noncustodial parent at a reasonable cost. Unless a custodial parent has satisfactory health insurance for the children other than Medicaid, he or she should petition the tribunal to include health insurance in new or modified support orders when health insurance is, or may be, available to the noncustodial parent at reasonable cost.

If a custodial parent has access to better health insurance, the support order may increase the noncustodial parent's obligation to offset the cost. Court orders can also be modified to include health care coverage.

States must have laws that should make medical support enforcement easier. For example, insurers can no longer refuse to enroll a child in a health care plan because the parents are not married or because the child does not live in the same household as the enrolled parent. In addition, child support agencies can require an employer to include a child on a medical insurance plan when the noncustodial parent participates in a group health plan but does not enroll the child.

This law provides that custodial parents can obtain information about coverage directly from an insurer, submit claims directly to the insurer, and be reimbursed directly by an insurer. For specific information about these laws in your state, contact the CSE office.

V. ENFORCEMENT

A main objective of the Child Support Enforcement (CSE) Program is to make sure that child support payments are made regularly and in the correct amount. While *noncustodial parents* who are involved in their children's lives are usually willing to pay child support, lapses of payment do occur. When they do, a family's budget can be quickly and seriously threatened. Some noncustodial parents do not pay regularly, and some spend a lot of effort and energy evading their responsibility for their children. The anxiety the *custodial parent* feels when payments are not regular can easily disrupt the family's life.

For this reason, Congress decided that *immediate income withholding* should be included in all child support orders. (States must also apply withholding to sources of income other than wages, such as commissions and bonuses; and to worker's compensation, disability, pension, or retirement benefits.) For child support orders issued or modified through state CSE Programs, immediate income withholding began on November 1, 1990. Immediate income withholding began January 1, 1994 for all initial orders that are not established through the CSE Program. The law allows for an exception to immediate income withholding if the *tribunal* finds good cause, or if both parents agree to an alternative arrangement. In these cases, if an *arrearage* equal to one month's payment occurs, that will automatically trigger withholding.

If the noncustodial parent has a regular job, income withholding for child support can be treated like other forms of payroll deduction, such as income tax, social security, union dues, or any other required payment.

If payments are skipped or stop entirely, especially if the noncustodial parent is self-employed, moves or changes jobs frequently, or works for cash or commissions, the CSE office will try to enforce the support order through other means. Subject to due process safeguards, states have laws which allow them to use enforcement techniques such as: state and Federal income tax offset, *liens* on real or personal property owned by the debtor, freezing of bank accounts, orders to withhold and deliver property to satisfy the debt, passport denial, or seizure and sale of property with the proceeds from the sale applied to the support debt.

These methods can be used by the CSE office without directly involving the courts.

All states have agreements with financial institutions doing business in their state for the purpose of conducting a quarterly data match known as the *Financial Institution Data Match (FIDM)*. The purpose of FIDM is to identify accounts belonging to non-custodial parents who are delinquent in their child support obligations. Once identified, these accounts may be subject to liens and levies issued by state or local child support enforcement agencies. An institution doing business in two or more states (*multi-state financial institution*) has the option to conduct the quarterly data match with OCSE or with the states where the institution does business. States are responsible for issuing levies to the financial institutions to collect the past-due child support.

Under the Passport Denial Program, states certify cases in which an obligor owes more than $2,500 in unpaid child support. The Office of Child Support Enforcement transmits the information to the Department of State so that a U.S. passport will not be issued, or renewed, to someone who is not supporting his or her children. Passports can be seized if the holder requests a change, such as a new address or an additional dependant. In some cases, the CSE agency can help to obtain a Federal warrant. The Department of State can then start procedures to revoke the passport or arrest the obligor at the border when he or she returns to the United States.

If actions available through the CSE program are not successful, state CSE agencies can take cases to court for other enforcement actions such as show cause hearings, contempt of court proceedings, and criminal prosecutions.

The noncustodial parent refuses to pay child support, but owns a good deal of property in the county. Can a lien be issued on the property?

Yes. However, a lien on property does not by itself result in the immediate collection of any money. It only prevents the owner from selling, transferring, or borrowing against the property until the child support debt is paid. Even so, the presence of a property lien may encourage the noncustodial parent to pay the past-due child support in order to get clear title to the property. States are now required to give full faith and credit to liens issued by another state.

Is it possible to collect the support payments from personal property?

Under some state laws, the enforcement official can issue an order to withhold and deliver. The order is sent to the person, company, or institution that is holding property belonging to the debtor, such as a bank account, investments, or personal property. The holder of the property must deliver it either to the enforcement agency or court that issued the support order. Some states permit the property to be attached or seized and sold to pay the debt. Some states require noncustodial parents with a poor payment history to pledge property as a guarantee of payment. Non-payment results in forfeiture of the property.

Can I have the income withholding applied to my existing child support order?

Yes, you can apply for the income withholding through your local CSE office or your attorney. Though there are limits on how much of a person's check can be withheld, income withholding can be used for both ongoing support and arrearages. Ask the CSE agency how this can be done.

Why can't my attorney work on my child support problem while I am receiving services from the child support program?

Your attorney can work with the child support program. For best results, the attorney and staff in the CSE agency should coordinate their efforts to prevent duplication of services and conflicting enforcement decisions.

My child's mother works for a big company and has moved several times in her job. Can income withholding work in this case?

Yes. States must recognize the income withholding orders from other states, and continue the income withholding as ordered, without regard to where the noncustodial parent or the custodial parent and children live.

My ex-husband has a good job and is willing to have the payments deducted from his paycheck, but his employer won't do it. What can I do?

Under every state's law, an employer **must** withhold the support if ordered to, or if the noncustodial parent requests it. If you run into problems with an employer, seek the assistance of your CSE office. The state CSE agency staff will send the employer a withholding notice which is binding on the employer. An employer who fails to withhold the income in accordance with the notice is liable for the accumulated amount that should have been withheld from the noncustodial parent's income. Employers who have questions about income withholding can find information and contacts on the Office of Child Support Enforcement (OCSE) website: http://www.acf.hhs.gov/programs/cse/newhire/employer/home.htm

The children's father works irregularly and is paid in cash. Income withholding won't work for me. What will?

Automatic billing, telephone reminders, and delinquency notices from your CSE office might convince him to make regular payments. Other techniques, such as property attachment, credit bureau reporting, tax refund offset, and liens might work for the arrearages. States can suspend or revoke drivers, professional, occupational, and recreational licenses if an arrearage develops. If none of these is successful, your enforcement office can take the case to court for stronger enforcement methods.

My ex-wife has her own computer programming service. How can the CSE office find out how much she earns, and how can they collect the money?

The CSE office has access to information from the Internal Revenue Service to determine her income and assets. This information will help to set the support order amount.

Cases involving self-employed noncustodial parents can be challenging to work, and often take more time and effort. If it is not possible to arrange for an allotment or withholding, it may be possible to secure liens on her payments from regular clients or to garnish her bank account. If her business depends on having a license, she may make arrangements to pay rather than risk losing her license. Knowing that arrears will be reported to a credit bureau may give her a strong incentive to comply with the order. Provide your caseworker with as much information as you can about the business and her clients.

My children's father owns a cross-country moving van. Why won't the child support office put a lien on it?

Most states will not attach property which a person needs to make a living. Talk to your caseworker about what kinds of property are available for liens and attachment in your state.

Can past-due child support be taken from the state income tax refund?

All states with state income tax must have laws that require the *offset* of state income tax refunds to collect past-due child support. The money first goes to satisfy current support due for that month, next for past-due support owed to families, and finally to states to repay cash assistance provided the family.

How does the non-paying parent find out that his or her state tax refund will be taken?

The state must notify the noncustodial parent in advance of taking the action. The notice specifies the amount owed in arrears and the amount to be offset. It also tells whom to contact if the person wants to contest the offset.

Can Federal income tax refunds be offset the same way?

Yes, states can request an offset of Federal tax refunds for past-due support over $500 owed to families on behalf of both minor and non-minor children, as well as over $150 owed to states that have provided assistance. States may choose how they distribute collections from Federal tax refund offsets. Some states pass some or all of the offset collections through to the family. Others apply some or all of the offset collections to money owed the state and Federal governments for assistance provided before they are distributed to families who are owed support.

My ex-spouse is in the Army. How do I go about having child support payments deducted from a paycheck? And can I get medical coverage for my child?

Members of the military are subject to the same income withholding requirements as other public or private employees. If a service member is not meeting a support obligation, an income withholding order can be sent to the Defense Finance and Accounting Service (DFAS) Center in Cleveland, Ohio. Ask your CSE office for information on how to start this action. There is information on the OCSE website at: http://www.acf.hhs.gov/programs/cse/fct/militaryguide2000.htm

DFAS also has useful child support information:
http://www.dfas.mil/militarypay/garnishment/supp-qa.html
http://www.dfas.mil/militarypay/garnishment.html

To get medical coverage for a child of a military member, the child must be enrolled in the Defense Enrollment Eligibility Reporting System (DEERS). There is information available at:
http://www.tricare.mil/deers/general.cfm

Contact the Defense Manpower Data Center support office for enrollment information.

800-334-4162 (California only)
800-527-5602 (Alaska and Hawaii only)
800-538-9552 (all other states)

My children's father retired from the Navy when he was only 40, just before our divorce. Can his military retirement check be garnished for back child support?

Yes, it is possible to garnish the income of retired members of the military. With the assistance of your caseworker or lawyer, you can get a garnishment order from the court and send it with a certified copy of your child support order to DFAS (as above). Your local enforcement office can tell you the exact procedures and follow through on your behalf.

The children's mother works for the Federal government. She was recently transferred and stopped making payments. What do I have to do to get them started again?

All Federal employees are subject to income withholding, and there is a central payment office for each Department, so moves within the Department should not affect an income withholding order. If you do not have a formal support order, ask a child support office or an attorney about establishing one. If you have a child support order, your CSE office or attorney can help you to secure payments by income withholding. If she has moved to a different Department, the Federal Parent Locator Service (FPLS) can provide her new location.

My child's father is a contractor who receives payments from the Federal Government. Can the Federal payments be seized for back child support?

Various types of payments can be seized through *Administrative Offset* to pay child support. They include both recurring and one-time payments. Types of payments that can be intercepted include payments to private vendors who perform work for a government agency, federal retirement payments, and relocation and travel reimbursements owed to federal employees. Some payments cannot be intercepted through this program. They include Veterans Affairs (VA) disability benefits, federal student loans, some Social Security payments, Railroad Retirement payments, Black Lung benefits, and payments made under certain programs based on financial need, or those that are excluded by the head of the Federal agency that administers them.

A case is eligible for an Administrative Offset when the non-custodial parent owes at least $25 in past due support and is at least 30 days delinquent in his or her child support payments. People who owe child support debts subject to Administrative Offset will be notified via a Pre-Offset Notice, which also includes information about the Federal Tax Refund Offset and Passport Denial programs. The Pre-Offset Notice also provides information about how to contest the debt amount.

States must submit to OCSE those cases that meet the criteria for the Federal Tax Refund Offset Program. The states use the same process to submit to the Administrative Offset Program. When a match occurs between the records of people who owe child support debts and the payment records for Federal payees, the *Financial Management Service (FMS)* in the Department of the Treasury will seize the amount and transmit it to the state, through OCSE. FMS will also send a notice to the non-custodial parent explaining the type of offset that occurred and referring him or her to the appropriate child support agency for further information.

The father of my child is in jail. Can I get support?

Past-due support may accumulate while the father is in jail. But unless he has assets, such as property, bank accounts, or any income such as wages from a work-release program, it is unlikely that support can be collected while he is in jail. You might write to the warden of the prison and ask if any provision is made for a prisoner to provide support for his children. Depending on state law, your support order may be modified so that payment is deferred or forgiven until he is released and working. (Some states will do this so that the arrearage when he is released is not so great that he might hide, but will seek work and resume payments.)

If he is in a Federal Correctional Facility, in addition to seizing available outside assets and income, if any, there also is a possibility that you can get child support payments from the inmate's prison account. According to the Bureau of Prisons instruction, the withdrawal of funds from an inmate's account is strictly voluntary. Child support obligations are listed as the fourth priority of funds that can be withdrawn. You, or your caseworker, will need to find out who the inmate's case manager is and write a letter to that person. Any correspondence to the case manager needs to specifically indicate that child support obligations are to be considered pursuant to the Inmate Financial Responsibility Program. If funds are not received, it may be due to the fact that the inmate has refused to make payment, or that the inmate is making payments that have priority over the child support payments. Contact with the case manager can verify whether or not the inmate is cooperating and willing to meet the child support obligations. (The Bureau of Prisons website has information about locating a prisoner: http://www.bop.gov/)

The children's father lost his job and is collecting unemployment compensation. Can child support payments be deducted and sent to me?

Yes. Unemployment compensation, and other state and Federal benefits can be tapped for child support. Ask your caseworker about the procedures, and make sure you tell your caseworker immediately if you learn about changes in the father's employment situation.

By my own calculation, my ex owes me $3,475 in past due child support. Can the enforcement agency try to collect it for me?

If this support was owed before the CSE office became involved in your case, the CSE office will have to verify the amount owed, and you may have to present evidence of the debt to a court before collection procedures can start. While the debt is being verified, the agency can try to collect support payments for current months.

I heard that my children's father is buying a very expensive car. He owes over $5,000 in back support. Can the credit agency be told this?

Yes. By law, the CSE office must periodically report the amount of past-due child support to credit reporting agencies. Consult your caseworker for more information.

The other parent does not work regularly and keeps falling behind in child support payments. Is there any way to establish regular payment?

As mentioned at the beginning of this section, property liens and attachments might work. In certain cases, state law also authorizes that the parent be required to post security, bond, or other guarantees to cover support obligations. These guarantees may be in the form of money or property. Ask your enforcement caseworker if other forms of payment might be applied to your case.

My ex-wife has declared bankruptcy and says she doesn't have to pay child support. Is that true?

Child support payments generally cannot be discharged in bankruptcy. This means that the parent who owed child support cannot escape this duty by filing for bankruptcy. As of October 1994, bankruptcies do not act as a *stay,* or hold, on actions to establish paternity or to establish or modify child support obligations. The relationship between child support and bankruptcy is complex, and you may need the help of someone familiar with bankruptcy law. Ask your caseworker how the CSE office can help.

My daughter's father says that since he gives her gifts and money he does not have to pay child support.

An order for support specifies how support is to be paid and gifts or payments made outside the order are generally not considered a credit against the ordered child support amount. If he is not paying as ordered, check with the CSE agency about enforcing the order. If you do not have a support order, you can talk with staff in the CSE agency about establishing one.

The child support office is not enforcing my case. Can I take it to a Federal Court?

If your caseworker and state CSE office have had no response to their requests for enforcement in another *jurisdiction,* it is possible for the case to be heard by a Federal court. This is not done often, and the decision to use a Federal court will be made by Federal investigators with help from the referring child support agency. The U.S. Attorney that has jurisdiction in your area makes the final decision about whether to prosecute. If you are not satisfied with the services you are receiving in your local CSE office, you may ask your state CSE agency for help. State agency addresses and phone numbers are listed at the end of this Handbook. They are also provided on our website, where we try to post changes as soon as we learn of them: http://ocse.acf.hhs.gov/int/directories/index.cfm?fuseaction=main.extivdl ist

In Section VI: Working Across Borders, there is information about Federal enforcement in cases in which the noncustodial parent lives in another state and is actively evading a support obligation.

My children are over 18 and don't get child support any more, but there is still a $10,000 arrearage owed to me for support that was never paid. Will the CSE office collect that money for me?

State *statutes of limitations* determine how long the CSE Office can try to collect on a child support debt. Within this period, the CSE office is required to collect verified back support. Ask your CSE office for more information.

Can my children be provided for if my ex-husband dies?

In most cases, the estate of the deceased noncustodial parent may only be responsible for satisfying any past-due support. In addition, the child may already be a beneficiary of that estate. See your local CSE office for assistance or guidance on filing an appropriate claim in probate court. Continued future support should be planned for by both parents and, in addition to verifying eligibility for Social Security and similar survivor benefits, parents should consider drafting appropriate wills and securing appropriate life insurance policies.

My ex-husband inherited a house and a sizeable amount of money from his parents. He already had some income and property. Now he doesn't have to work, and he put everything into his brother's name and got his child support reduced to the state minimum.

His action may constitute a "fraudulent transfer." Check with the state CSE agency to see if it would be considered as such under state law and if the property transfer can be voided. In addition, courts can establish a support order based on imputed income -- the amount that someone would be able to pay if he or she had not voluntarily lowered his income or transferred his or her assets. Your CSE agency can provide information about a possible review of the order if the amount was reduced because of his actions.

My case is difficult and the state is having a hard time collecting from my ex-spouse. I'm thinking about contacting a private collection agency. What information is available about them?

A private collection agency (PCA) is a privately owned, for-profit business that, for a fee, helps parents collect child support. OCSE recognizes a parent's right to choose to work with a PCA. However, parents should make informed choices. If you hire a PCA, make sure that you understand your rights and obligations under the contract before you sign. If you have access to the internet at home or at a public library, OCSE has developed an Information Memorandum that includes information that you might consider if you are thinking of using a PCA. http://www.acf.hhs.gov/programs/cse/pol/IM/im-02-09a.htm

Do I have to close my case with the state CSE agency to hire a PCA?

The state cannot require you to close your case simply because you hired a PCA. A PCA may require that you close your case with the state as a condition of your contract. If you do close your case with the state, the following collections services may not be available: tracking changes in the noncustodial parent's employment through the National Directory of New Hires; interception of state and Federal tax refunds and lottery winnings; passport denial; and license revocation or suspension.

VI. DISTRIBUTION

It is important that families receive their child support payments as quickly as possible. Any delay can quickly and seriously threaten a family's budget. For this reason, states are required to distribute most payments within two days of their receipt. When two states are involved, each one must send payments out within two days. Each state has established *a State Disbursement Unit (SDU)* -- a single unit to receive and send out payments for child support. These SDUs are intended to get payments out with a minimum of turnaround time. They have the additional advantage of providing a single place in the state to which employers can send child support payments collected from their employees.

State SDUs are responsible for:

- receipt and disbursement of all payments;

- accurate identification of payments;

- prompt disbursement of the custodial parent's share of any payment;

- furnishing to any parent, upon request, timely information on the current status of payments under a support order; and

- maintaining a statewide record of support orders.

Families who receive public assistance under the *Temporary Assistance to Needy Families (TANF)* program, must assign their right to child support to the state. States have the option to "pass through" child support collections to families who receive TANF ($100 for 1 child/$200 for 2 or more children) without reducing the assistance payment.

After the family leaves the assistance program, the total current support collection goes to the family. Amounts collected beyond the amount ordered as current support are considered to be payments towards arrearages owed to the family and/or to the state/Federal Government.

Under current laws, families receive their post-assistance arrears before the state collects money to repay the government for the assistance payments.

Will I receive the entire amount of support paid?

If you have not received cash assistance, you will receive the total child support payment (less any fees the state may collect). If you are receiving cash assistance, check with your state CSE agency. Some states will pass some or all of the child support payments through to you. Others will use the entire amount to repay the money provided to your family. If you are not receiving cash assistance now but did in the past, and if amounts are still owed to the state, any support collected beyond the amount ordered for current support and for arrearages owed to you may be used to reduce the arrearages owed to the state.

I am working with a private collection service. Can the collection agency ask to have my child support payments sent there?

Orders established after 1993 require that wage withholdings are sent through the State Disbursement Unit (SDU). State IV-D programs can send payments in the custodial parent's name to the address that he or she provides, including a private agency that you delegate to be the agent of your child for collection purposes, unless otherwise prohibited by state law.

My child's father told me weeks ago that his tax refund was taken for child support. When will I get the money?

It usually takes three to five weeks from the time the money is offset from the obligor's tax refund until the state receives it. The Department of the Treasury has encouraged states to hold collections from joint tax returns for up to six months in case the obligor's spouse who does not owe child support files for his or her share of the refund. The Office of Child Support Enforcement and Treasury Department will be working together to provide information to the states if the spouse has filed a claim for his or her part of the refund and has received the money. States will be able to distribute the offset to the family when they receive that information. Check with your CSE agency to see if the money has been collected and, if so, when you can expect to receive it.

VII. ACF HEALTHY MARRIAGE INITIATIVE

The U.S. DHHS Administration for Children and Families (ACF) Healthy Marriage Initiative began in 2003. Its mission is to help couples who choose to get married to gain greater access to marriage education services that will enable them to acquire the skills and knowledge necessary to form and sustain a healthy marriage.

Research indicates that children in stable two-parent families do better, on average, than those from single-parent households. Section 1115 of the Social Security Act (Act) authorizes the Secretary to test new uses of child support funds if he determines that these uses are likely to further the objectives of the Act, improve the financial well-being of children, or otherwise improve the operation of the child support program.

Section 1115 authorizes the Secretary to conduct demonstration projects designed to meet the objectives of the Child Support Enforcement program, such as:

- locating absent parents;

- establishing paternity when needed;

- establishing child support orders; and

- enforcing child support orders when needed.

One of the main activities of the demonstration projects will be teaching skills to help couples to communicate better, manage their emotions more effectively when they disagree and be better parents for their children. Skills that help parents work cooperatively should also increase voluntary paternity establishment for children born out of wedlock. Even when couples are unable to sustain a healthy marriage, parents who can work together are more likely to agree to fair support orders and to provide financial and emotional support for their children.

What is the connection between Child Support Enforcement and the ACF Healthy Marriage Initiative?

The purpose of the Healthy Marriage Initiative is to test new strategies in communities to strengthen the child support program's ability to promote the financial well-being of children by integrating healthy marriage and healthy parental relationship skills building into the existing range of child support enforcement activities. Funded projects will provide information and skills primarily to couples with children who are considering marriage. It is important for unmarried parents to realize that voluntarily establishing paternity is a giant step towards ensuring that a child can depend on both parents. It is not the beginning of an adversarial child support proceeding. These programs will explain to parents that paternity establishment does not mean abandoning the hope of marriage. Couples can get the information and skills they need to make good decisions about getting married and establishing paternity. These are compatible actions, both of which are important aspects of taking responsibility for one's family.

Will funding of these projects divert funds from establishing and collecting child support?

No. There is no reduction in the amount of Federal or state funds dedicated to supporting the services currently being provided by the IV-D program to families and children as a result of these projects. The Federal funds for the project will add to the total being spent on the IV-D program. The state funds to provide matches for these federal funds are donated funds. They do not come from state child support enforcement agency funds that would otherwise be used to operate the child support program. Section 1115 allows the Department of Health and Human Services to treat donated funds as state funds to be matched with the federal funds.

How will the outcomes of these projects be measured?

These projects are designed to produce positive outcomes, but it is precisely the purpose of Section 1115 projects to test ideas that hold the promise of increasing paternity establishment and financial support of children. The Department will conduct a comprehensive, high quality evaluation to assess just how these programs affect families and children, and the operation of the Child Support Program. The evaluation will be designed in partnership with research organizations, academic researchers, foundations and the states and local entities conducting the projects.

Does the Healthy Marriage Initiative risk pushing women into unhealthy marriages?

No. Healthy marriage projects are intended to help people form healthy and respectful relationships and marriages that reduce the risk of abuse and violence. Domestic abuse and violence are serious problems. Healthy marriage projects do not push people into marriages, but help them understand how healthy relationships and marriages work and help them assess their own relationships realistically. All ACF supported activities must include appropriate attention to potential issues of domestic violence, and every opportunity must be taken to ensure the safety of victims or potential victims.

VIII. WORKING ACROSS BORDERS

COOPERATION BETWEEN STATES, TRIBES, COUNTRIES

Interstate/Inter-jurisdictional Enforcement

It has been difficult to collect child support when the parent obligated to pay child support lives in one *jurisdiction* and the child and custodial parent live in another. However, all state and tribal *IV-D Child Support Enforcement* (CSE) agencies are required to pursue child support enforcement, including location, paternity establishment, and establishment of support obligations, as vigorously for children who live outside their borders as for those under their own jurisdiction.

With the enactment of the *Full Faith and Credit for Child Support Orders Act*, and the Federal mandate that all states enact the *Uniform Interstate Family Support Act (UIFSA)*, interstate enforcement of child support obligations is improving. Tribes have not been required to enact UIFSA in order to receive Federal funding for child support programs as states have been required to do. However courts of all United States territories, states and tribes must accord full faith and credit to a child support order issued by another state or tribe that had jurisdiction over the parties and the subject matter. UIFSA includes a provision designed to ensure that, when more than one state is involved, there is only one valid child support order which can be enforced for current support. The law also includes a provision that allows a IV-D agency to work a case involving an out-of-jurisdiction obligor directly if certain conditions are met.

UIFSA has procedures under which an enforcement official (or private attorney) can refer a case to another tribunal within the United States. The laws can be used to establish paternity and to establish, modify, or enforce a support order.

Interstate *income withholding* can be used to enforce a support order in another jurisdiction if the *noncustodial parent's* employer is known. Under UIFSA, income withholding can be initiated in one state and sent directly to an employer in another without involving the CSE agency in that state. Laws vary and you will need to ask your caseworker whether this option is available in your case.

State CSE Agencies all have an office called the Central Registry to receive incoming interstate child support cases, ensure that the information given is complete, send cases to the right local office, and respond to inquiries from out-of-jurisdiction CSE offices. Standard forms make it easier for state and tribal caseworkers to find the information they need to enforce a case, and to be sure they are supplying enough information for another jurisdiction to enforce their case.

I know the out-of-state address of my children's father, and my caseworker sent a petition to establish my support order there. That was three months ago, and still no support payments. What's wrong?

It may be any number of things: enforcement officials may not be able to serve notice on the noncustodial parent due to inadequate address information; if a hearing is necessary, it may take a while to get a court date. Generally speaking, a state must complete service of process to begin an action within 90 days of locating the noncustodial parent, and the majority of orders should be established within six months from the date of service of process. Continue to keep in touch with your caseworker to resolve any delay or to provide any new information you may have.

I need to establish paternity for my child, and the father lives in another part of the country. How does this work?

The fact that you and the person presumed to be the father live in different jurisdictions will not keep you from pursuing a paternity establishment action. Your state may be able to claim jurisdiction and establish paternity if the father has lived there, the child was conceived in your state, or there is another basis for the exercise of personal jurisdiction. Otherwise your state can petition the other jurisdiction to establish paternity under their laws. Often, genetic tests will be ordered to help prove paternity. Ask your caseworker for specific information about the laws in your state and the state where the other parent lives.

My caseworker filed an interstate petition for paternity. The father denied it, and the other court just dismissed the case. What went wrong?

A responding CSE office should not dismiss a case without asking for the information it needs. The initiating state is required to provide that information within 30 days. (Tribal IV-D agencies do not have this requirement.) Either party in a contested paternity action can request blood or genetic testing. Ask your caseworker to reopen the case. You have the right to establish paternity until your child's 18th birthday.

If paternity is established in another state, will the support order also be entered in that state?

Yes, UIFSA procedures cover establishing paternity and establishing and enforcing child support orders when more than one tribunal is involved. Ask your caseworker how this is done.

Will location and enforcement services cost more if my agency is dealing with another state or jurisdiction? I am not receiving cash assistance.

Possibly. It depends on what the CSE office has to do to find the noncustodial parent and to establish regular payment. The more solid information and leads you provide, the more efficiently your case can be conducted. For non-assistance cases, service fees vary in different states. Your caseworker should be able to tell you more about these costs in your particular case. (See discussion in the Introduction section of this Handbook.)

I don't have a support order. Can I have one established by petitioning the court where my ex-husband lives?

Yes. This can also be done by your CSE office. Depending on the facts, it could be handled in your jurisdiction or referred to another jurisdiction under UIFSA. An affidavit of the facts, indicating the name and address of the responsible parent, details of your financial circumstances, and the needs of the child, will be included. The petition will be mailed to the enforcement agency, the court, or the interstate official where the father lives. The responding jurisdiction will review this information together with information about the father's ability to pay, and set the amount to be paid.

I have had to wait several months for my enforcement agency to get a reply to its request for location assistance in another state. Why does it take so long to get an answer?

Even though they try to be responsive, enforcement agencies have a very high demand for their services. An agency's ability to act rapidly depends on the characteristics of the case, the quality of information received, and the amount of staff and other resources they have to devote to it. Be sure to follow up regularly with your caseworker to make sure that each jurisdiction is actively working your case.

As soon as the children's father is notified about enforcement, he moves. How will I ever be able to collect my support?

It is difficult to enforce child support payments when the noncustodial parent intentionally moves to avoid paying. Try to be an active participant in your own case. Whenever you learn that the noncustodial parent has moved or has a new job, you should tell your caseworker as soon as possible. All states are required to have a State Directory of New Hires, and employers are required to report hiring new employees within 20 days. The information, in turn, is sent to a National Directory of New Hires. This helps locate the noncustodial parent quickly if he/she moves on to a new job.

Isn't there a law now that makes it a Federal crime to not pay child support if the child lives in another state?

The Child Support Recovery Act of 1992 (CSRA) made it a Federal crime to willfully fail to pay support for a child living in another state if the arrearages exceed $5,000 or are unpaid for longer than a year. That law was strengthened in 1998 by Public Law 105-187, which added new categories of felonies with stronger penalties for more blatant child support evaders. Because successful prosecution depends on extensive investigation, the U. S. Attorney's offices are very selective about the cases they accept. Priority is given to cases: (1) where there is a pattern of moving from state to state to avoid payment; (2) where there is a pattern of deception (e.g., use of false name or Social Security number);

(3) where there is failure to make support payments after being held in contempt of court; and (4) where failure to make support payments is connected to some other Federal offense such as bankruptcy fraud. The U. S. Attorneys may also require that it can be shown that the nonpayer has financial resources and is able to pay.

In nearly all cases, U.S. Attorneys ask that cases be reviewed and forwarded to them by state CSE offices. When a CSE office has screened and referred the case, the U.S. Attorneys can be reasonably sure of receiving significant information about the case and that civil and state criminal remedies are exhausted. Check with your caseworker to see if prosecution under this Act would be available in your case. The final decision about whether to prosecute is with the U.S. Attorney, relying heavily on information provided by the CSE agency.

My former wife lives in another state. She owns an expensive car, jewelry, and several pieces of property. Would the CSE Program be able to attach this property for child support?

An interstate CSE action may be filed on your behalf to ask the other state to attach this property.

The children's mother lives in another state and every time the kids come home from there, they talk about her new car or stove or something, but she still won't pay her child support. Why can she get credit if the courts know she owes her kids so much?

CSE office staff must report child support arrearages to credit bureaus, so that information is available to people/offices that offer credit. Also, the state notifies the noncustodial parent if the debt will be reported to the credit-reporting network. Sometimes, that is enough to encourage payment of the overdue support.

Tribal Cases

The Department of Health and Human Services recognizes the unique relationship between the Federal government and Federally recognized Indian tribes, and acknowledges this special government-to-government relationship in the implementation of the tribal provisions of the Personal Responsibility and Work Opportunity Reconciliation Act (PRWORA).

For the first time in the history of the title *IV-D program*, PRWORA authorized tribes and *tribal organizations* to operate child support enforcement programs like states do.

Before enactment of PRWORA, only the states were authorized to administer IV-D services. However, within much of tribal territory, the authority of state and local governments is limited or non-existent. The Constitution, numerous court decisions, and Federal law clearly reserve to tribes important powers of self-government, including the authority to make and enforce laws, to *adjudicate* civil and criminal disputes including domestic relations cases, to tax, and to license. States have been limited in their ability to provide IV-D services on tribal lands and Native American families have had difficulty obtaining services from state IV-D programs. Cooperative agreements between tribes and states have helped bring child support services to increasing numbers of Indian and Alaska Native families.

The tribes that are operating child support programs at the time of the printing of this Handbook are listed at the end of the booklet. Tribal programs are also listed on our website at: http://ocse3.acf.hhs.gov/int/directories/tribaldirectors.cfm

My ex-husband is a Native American who lives and works on an Indian reservation. Can the CSE Program help get child support for my children?

If your ex-husband is a member of a tribe with a IV-D program, this will not be a problem. The state office should contact the tribal IV-D office and work cooperatively with them to get the child support you need. You may also want to consider applying for child support services directly from the tribal child support office.

If your ex-husband is a member of a tribe that does not have an agreement with OCSE to operate a CSE program, your caseworker should contact the tribal court and ask about the tribal procedures for child support. Most tribes have an office that handles child support enforcement cases even if they do not have a cooperative agreement with OCSE to operate a child support enforcement program.

My ex-husband is not a Native American, but he works on a reservation. Will his employer withhold income from his check to make the child support payment?

If the tribe is operating a IV-D CSE program, your caseworker should send the income withholding order through the tribal IV-D agency. The tribal IV-D agency will present the income withholding order to the tribal enterprise for processing and income withholding.

If the tribe does not have an agreement with OCSE to operate a child support enforcement program, your caseworker should contact the tribal court and ask about the tribal procedures for honoring an income withholding order. In most instances, the tribal enterprise will honor the withholding order, but it must be processed through the tribe's procedures.

I am a Native American mother of a three-year-old and I live on a reservation. His father is not Native American, does not live on the reservation, and does not fall under the jurisdiction of the tribal court. How can I get him to help support his son?

If your tribe has a CSE agency, work through that office to establish and enforce an order. You can also apply for child support services with the appropriate state office. There is nothing to preclude you from applying for services with both the tribe and the state. States and tribes are working cooperatively to ensure that the children get the support that they need.

International Cases

The father of my child has left the United States. How can I get my court order for child support enforced?

The U.S. Government has negotiated Federal-level reciprocity declarations with several countries and is negotiating declarations with others on behalf of all U.S. jurisdictions. Our website lists countries with which the US has agreements at:
http://www.acf.hhs.gov/programs/cse/international/index.html

If there is not a Federal-level agreement, check with your state CSE agency. Many state CSE agencies have agreements with foreign countries to recognize child support judgments made in other countries. Our Intergovernmental Referral Guide includes information given to us by the states about countries that they work with at:

https://extranet.acf.hhs.gov/irgauth/login

These international child support agreements specify procedures for establishing and enforcing child support orders across borders. While requirements for getting enforcement action may vary depending on the other nation involved, a parent will be asked to provide the same information as in a domestic case, including as much specific information, such as address and employer of the noncustodial parent, as is possible.

If the noncustodial parent works for an American company, or for a foreign company with offices in the United States, income withholding might work even if the country he or she lives in does not have any agreement to enforce an American state's order. Even in cases where the noncustodial parent is living and working in a country that has no reciprocity agreement, approaching the foreign employer directly for help might prove successful.

I checked with the CSE office, but my daughter's father lives in a country that has no agreement with any state to enforce child support obligations. Is there anything else to try?

The Office of Citizens Consular Services may be able to give you information about how to have the support order enforced in that country and how to obtain a list of attorneys there. That address is: Department of State, Office of Citizens Consular Services, Washington, D.C. 20520.

My child's mother is still in this country, but I understand that she is planning to live abroad with her new husband. She owes me $14,000 in child support. Is there anything the CSE Office can do?

States certify cases in which an obligor owes more than $2,500 in unpaid child support to the Secretary of Health and Human Services, who, in turn, will transmit the certification to the Secretary of State for denial of passports. The passport can also be seized if she asks for any change -- change of address, a new visa, addition of a child, etc. In addition, you should ask your caseworker if the court can impose a bond to secure payment of the arrears and future support.

IX. NONCUSTODIAL PARENTS' RIGHTS AND RESPONSIBILITIES

Both research and observation give clear and convincing evidence that children benefit greatly if both parents are actively involved in their lives. It is critical to children as they grow and develop. Bringing a child into the world means making a commitment to care for him or her throughout childhood – ensuring the best possible environment to grow in. Children need safe places to live, nourishing food, education, and a solid foundation of values. Mothers and fathers bring different, but equally important, qualities to their children. In a divorce or non-marital situation, either parent may be granted custody of the child -- or both may share equally in the physical custody and/or decision-making responsibilities.

Because traditionally men are less likely to have custody, and because the role of fathers is so important, the Department of Health and Human Services (HHS) has established a Fatherhood website at: http://fatherhood.hhs.gov/index.shtml

I'm getting a divorce and my spouse wants me to pay child support directly to her. Can I insist on paying through the CSE office?

A noncustodial parent can apply for child support services if the case is not being enforced through the Child Support Enforcement (CSE) program, unless the support order requires you to pay her directly. Since January 1994, support orders must include a provision for *income withholding* unless both parents and the courts agree on another payment method. If your order does not call for income withholding, you can request this service. If you do, you will have a record that you have made payments as required. If you are self-employed, you may be able to arrange for an automatic transfer of funds to the child support agency through *electronic funds transfer* (EFT*)*. Either parent can apply for CSE services, which include collecting and distributing payments.

I'm the noncustodial parent. I love my kids. I pay my child support. About half the time when I go to pick them up for my weekend, my ex-wife has made other plans for them. It's not fair that the state will enforce my child support obligation but not do anything about my right to see my kids.

Although the CSE Program lacks authority to enforce visitation, many state or local governments have developed procedures for enforcing visitation orders. Also, the Federal government has made funding available to states for developing model programs to ensure that children will be able to have the continuing care and emotional support of both parents. Check with your local CSE agency and clerk of court to see what resources are available to you and to find out about laws that address custody and visitation.

After I pay my child support, I don't even have enough money for decent food. When my child support order was set, I was making about $300 a month more than I am now. Can I get the order changed?

Either parent can request a review, and adjustment, if appropriate, of a child support obligation at least every 36 months, or sooner if there has been a substantial change in circumstances such as reduced income of the obligated parent or a change in medical support provisions. Check with your CSE office to see if your child support obligation is in line with state guidelines and ask how to request a review.

If your case does not meet the state's standards for review, either because the order has been reviewed within your state's review period or the change in income is smaller than would merit an adjustment under state standards, you may still be able to petition the courts for a hearing. In this case, it may be helpful to have the services of an attorney. Your local legal aid society may be able to advise you about finding low-cost counsel if you cannot afford a private attorney. Also, a number of states have information about how to handle your case _pro se_ (a legal term for representing yourself) to have the courts determine if your support obligation should be changed. Contact your local CSE office or the clerk of the court for more information.

Is there a limit to the amount of money that can be taken from my paycheck for child support?

The amount that can be withheld from an employee's wages is limited by the Federal Consumer Credit Protection Act (FCCPA) to 50 percent of *disposable income* if an obligated parent has a second family and 60 percent if there is no second family. These limits are each increased by 5 percent (to 55% and 65%) if payments are in arrears for a period equal to 12 weeks or more. State law may further limit the amount that can be taken from a wage earner's paycheck.

I can't find my child and the custodial parent. What can I do?

One of the services of the Office of Child Support Enforcement is helping to locate children in parental kidnapping cases. Federal law allows the use of the Federal Parent Locator Service (FPLS) in parental kidnapping or child custody cases (including cases in which the custodial parent has hidden the child in violation of a visitation order) if: 1) a civil action to make or enforce a custody order has been filed in the state courts; or 2) a criminal custodial interference case is being investigated or prosecuted.

Requests for information from the FPLS in custody and parental kidnapping cases must come from a state CSE agency. State CSE agency telephone numbers and addresses are at: https://ocse.acf.hhs.gov/int/directories/index.cfm?fuseaction=main.extivd list (English) https://ocse.acf.hhs.gov/int/directories/index.cfm?fuseaction=main.ext/Es panolIVDAll (Spanish)

State CSE agency web site links are available on our web site at: http://www.acf.dhhs.gov/programs/cse/extinf.html

States may collect a fee from people using the service to cover processing costs.

I just found out that I was named the father of a child I never even knew about. How can that happen and what can I do about it?

If you have received papers naming you as the father of a child, and providing information about attending a hearing, contacting the CSE agency or some other tribunal, or other action that you must take, it is very important to follow up as required by the document you received. Check with the CSE agency to see how to request genetic testing, or to learn about paternity establishment in your state.

There are cases in which a man can be determined to be the father of a child if he was "properly served" notice of a paternity hearing but did not go. What constitutes "proper service" is determined by the state – it may be in the form of a registered letter, a notice delivered to the person's legal residence, or even a notice published in the newspaper. Check with the CSE agency in the state where paternity was established to see what can be done. If the paternity was established by fraud, duress, or material mistake of fact, it may be possible, depending on state law, to challenge the paternity finding.

Also, there are cases in which the alleged father is misidentified – if names are closely similar, for example. There, too, your best information about resolving this will come from the state CSE agency. Contact information is at the end of this Handbook if it was not provided in the notice that you received about the paternity.

How long do I have to pay?

Emancipation and the age of majority for termination of child support are determined by the states. Some states have provision for child support payments while a child is in college. If you have access to the internet, there is state-specific information on our web site, at

https://extranet.acf.hhs.gov/irgauth/login

You can also check with the state CSE agency. Telephone numbers and addresses are listed at the end of the Handbook.

For particular situations -- if a child leaves school before reaching the age of majority, is still in school but is emancipated, or is enrolled but not attending classes, for example -- check with the child support agency to see how the state handles them.

If a child is handicapped, parents may be required to pay support after that child becomes an adult.

I pay child support every month. I buy extras like school clothes and pay for field trips. Why can't I claim my child as a dependent?

Under domestic relations tax provisions set forth by the Internal Revenue Code, for divorced or separated parents, the parent who has custody for a greater portion of the calendar year is entitled to the dependency exemption for the child (See 26 U.S.C. 152(e). In some cases, a court or administrator will address the issue of who can claim the dependency. Also, the parent with custody can provide the other parent with a written statement that he/she may take the exemption for a given year. The noncustodial parent can then attach the statement to the income tax form, using IRS Form 8332, and claim the child(ren) as dependents for a given tax year. To obtain IRS Form 8332 and other IRS Forms and Publications, visit the IRS Web site at
http://www.irs.gov/forms_pubs/index.html

In the case of parents who have never married, the IRS gives information about who can be claimed as a dependent in their Form 501:
http://www.irs.gov/publications/index.html
Generally, that would be a child for whom you had provided more than 50% of the support over the year.

My current wife is working and when we filed our taxes, the whole refund was taken.

If a couple filed a joint return and only one of them is liable for child support payments, in non-community property states the other spouse can file an amended return to receive his or her share of the tax refund. The person who is not responsible for the child support debt can file tax Form 8379, the Injured Spouse Claim and Allocation. You can get Form 8379 by calling the IRS (listed in your telephone directory) or by visiting the Treasury Department's website at: http://www.irs.ustreas.gov.

Follow the instructions on Form 8379 carefully and provide the required documents.

I tried to get a passport for a business trip abroad. The State Department denied it because of child support. I don't know which state said I owe child support.

If you do not know which state certified your case, or if you have never owed back child support, check the list provided with the Department of State denial letter for the contact information it gives for the state where you currently live. If you don't have the list, staff in the state agency can check with the Federal Office of Child Support Enforcement to see which state certified the case and can get you contact information for resolving any problem. State agency addresses and telephone numbers are at the back of this Handbook.

X. LESSONS LEARNED

The Child Support Enforcement Program was established as a part of the Department of Health and Human Services (HHS) in 1975 with the objective of ensuring that children receive financial support from parents who are not living in their household. Since then, four general types of noncustodial parents have emerged:

- those who are willing and able to pay,
- those who are willing but unable,
- those who are unwilling but able, and
- those who are unwilling and unable to provide support for their children.

Learning to work with these groups is changing the program's ability to collect child support and its attitude about other ways to help children and families.

Parents who are willing and able to pay support have their children's best interests at heart. These children likely will flourish and grow to responsible adulthood. If the parents miss a payment, a caseworker's early telephone call will often reveal the reason – a change of job or other circumstance, an error in payment identification – and the problem usually can be resolved.

For parents who are willing but unable to pay, a number of states have started programs for teaching job skills or finding employment. States are looking at the benefits of ensuring that child support orders are set at a realistic amount. Many states work with these parents effectively to ensure that child support debt does not drive them away from their children.

Parents who are unwilling but able to pay face strong enforcement tools, such as wage withholding, tax offset, passport denial, and asset seizures. Just as important, parents who have a close relationship with their children are more inclined to pay child support: removing barriers to access may lead to increased collections, and to a better chance for children to have a secure, successful adulthood.

For parents who are unwilling and unable to pay, an ideal program would give them the skills to earn enough money to support their children and help them discover the satisfaction of parenting. Setting fair support orders and helping these people acquire job and parenting skills might help them to make their children's lives, and their own, more rewarding.

To help reach its ideal, the program has several efforts under way. We want to make it as easy as possible for children to have the love and the financial support of both their parents. We want to ensure that child support orders are fair -- that noncustodial parents are not burdened by a debt they cannot pay -- and that children receive the support that their parents can afford. We want to ensure that people who bring a child into the world shoulder the responsibility that it entails.

Children need two involved parents:

Over the last four decades, the number of children growing up in homes without fathers has dramatically increased. In 1960, fewer than 10 million children did not live with their fathers. Today, the number is nearly 25 million. More than one-third of these children will not see their fathers at all during the course of a year. Studies show that children who grow up without responsible fathers are significantly more likely to experience poverty, perform poorly in school, engage in criminal activity, and abuse drugs and alcohol. Purely from the point of view of ensuring financial support, research suggests that there is a positive relationship between noncustodial fathers' involvement with their children and their payment of child support.

HHS supports programs and policies that reflect the critical role that both fathers and mothers play in building strong and successful families and in the well-being of children. Some programs reach out directly to fathers to promote responsible fatherhood and strengthen parenting skills. Other programs work to discourage young men from becoming fathers until they are married and ready for the responsibility. HHS also partners with states and with faith-based and community organizations to promote responsible fatherhood in local communities nationwide. And HHS researches the role that responsible fathers play in ensuring the healthy development of children. More information about many HHS initiatives promoting fatherhood is available at http://fatherhood.hhs.gov.

Since fiscal year 1997, $10 million has been available each year for grants to all 50 states, the District of Columbia, Puerto Rico, the Virgin Islands and Guam to promote access and visitation programs to increase noncustodial parents' involvement in their children's lives. Each state has flexibility in how it designs and operates these programs and may use these funds to provide such services as voluntary or mandatory mediation, counseling, education, development of parenting plans, visitation enforcement (including monitoring, supervision, and neutral drop-off and pick-up), and development of guidelines for visitation and alternative custody arrangements.

The 1996 welfare reform law recognized that two-parent, married families represent the ideal environment for raising children and therefore featured a variety of family formation provisions. HHS has approved grants and waivers for responsible fatherhood efforts designed to help noncustodial fathers support their children financially and emotionally. Under the Partners for Fragile Families demonstration, 10 states are testing ways for child support enforcement programs and community and faith-based organizations to work together to help young unmarried fathers obtain employment, provide financial support to their families, and improve parenting skills. Eight states have also received demonstration grants or waivers to allow them to test comprehensive approaches to encourage more responsible fathering by noncustodial parents. In addition, President George W. Bush's Welfare Reform Reauthorization proposal includes up to $300 million for programs that encourage healthy, stable marriages. These programs would incorporate research and technical assistance into promising approaches that work and may involve premarital education and counseling efforts.

Child support orders should be fair:

Child support orders that are set too high relative to low-income obligors' ability to pay contribute to child support arrears and, unfortunately, child support debt can drive a wedge between a parent and child. A number of states' guideline formulas rely on a "self-support reserve" for the basic living expenses of a noncustodial parent before a child support obligation is determined. The self-support reserve in most states, if it is used at all, can be considerably below the Federal poverty level for one person.

Another cause of child support orders not matching a parent's ability to pay is the establishment of orders by default. Default orders are written if a noncustodial parent fails to appear in the child support case being brought against him or her. All too often, a noncustodial parent will not get the notice of the proceeding, or will not understand that a fairer order might be written if he or she attends the hearing.

OCSE, with our various colleague agencies, is studying effective policies and practices for working with low-income noncustodial parents. Studies by the HHS Office of the Inspector General and others report on the large percentage of total arrears owed by low-income parents who may never have the resources to satisfy their debt. Preliminary outcomes have already reinforced beliefs that the most effective way to avoid arrears for low-income noncustodial parents is to make sure that they are a part of the order establishment process and that the process ends with a reasonable obligation.

States also may need to maximize access to and use of computerized wage data to find as much earnings information as possible for all cases, including cases established by default, and those in which a parent tries to hide income. Designing a system that sets fair and reasonable obligations to encourage rather than discourage child support payment will go a long way toward reaching that goal.

Enforcement, when required, should be effective:

In addition to actions that can be taken through law enforcement and judicial proceedings (such as citations for contempt of court, and filing of state and Federal criminal charges), over the years, Congress has provided the Child Support Enforcement Program with strong enforcement tools including: wage withholding, offsetting of Federal and state income tax refunds, and the ability to secure liens on property. In recent years, more tools have been added:

An expanded Federal Parent Locator Service: Provisions in the 1996 bipartisan welfare reform legislation established a *Federal Case Registry* and *National Directory of New Hires* to track delinquent parents across state lines. This legislation also required that employers report all new hires to state agencies for transmittal to the national directory and expanded and streamlined procedures for direct withholding of child support from wages.

Financial Institution Data Matching: In 1998, Congress made it easier for multi-state institutions to match records by using the Federal Office of Child Support Enforcement. Accounts of non-payers can be seized or frozen to help satisfy a child support debt.

Project Save Our Children: An initiative on criminal child support enforcement, Project Save Our Children, is succeeding in its pursuit of chronic delinquent parents who owe large sums of child support. Multi-agency regional task forces, involving Federal and state law enforcement agencies, work together to obtain convictions in interstate cases.

Passport Denial: The State Department is notified for passport denial when a parent falls $2,500 behind in child support payments. If that person applies for a passport, or tries to renew or update it, the passport will be denied until the state that submitted the case is satisfied that the debt is paid or a satisfactory plan is agreed to.

As you can see, we continue to learn new lessons with every passing year. We hope the Child Support Enforcement Program will serve the families who need it well: that children will have all of the love and the support -- both emotional and financial -- that both parents, working together, can provide for them.

XI. CONCLUSION

The success you have in obtaining regular, adequate, and full child support payments can often depend on how well you can make the child support enforcement system work for you. At the same time, it is important to remember that not all the solutions to your child support problems are within your control. The legal rights and welfare of all parties must be carefully guarded, and sometimes laws that protect the rights of one parent seem unfair to the other.

Knowledge is power. The more you know about child support enforcement procedures where you and the noncustodial parent live, the better you will be able to exercise your rights and responsibilities under the law, and the more successful you will be in obtaining the support that rightfully belongs to your children. As you proceed with your enforcement case, it is a good idea to keep a written account of the actions taken and the outcomes of those actions. Do not hesitate to ask questions and make suggestions to your enforcement caseworker. If you are not satisfied with the actions taken on your behalf, you have recourse to appeal your case to the head of the local CSE office as well as to the director of the state or tribal Child Support Enforcement agency. Keep in mind that it is always best to communicate the problem in writing.

An informed parent can help make the child support enforcement system work. This, together with improvements that state enforcement programs, legislatures, and the courts are making, can benefit millions of parents and their children.

APPENDIX

GLOSSARY OF CHILD SUPPORT ENFORCEMENT TERMS

Adjudication – the entry of a judgment, decree, or order by a judge or other decision-maker, based on the evidence submitted by the parties.

Administration for Children and Families (ACF) – the agency in the Department of Health and Human Services that houses the Office of Child Support Enforcement.

Administrative offset – seizure of a tax refund or other Federal payment to satisfy a child support debt.

Administrative procedure – method by which support orders are made and enforced by an executive agency rather than by courts and judges.

Agent of the child – person, usually a parent, who has the legal authority to act on behalf of a minor.

Arrearage – unpaid child support for past periods owed by a parent who is obligated to pay.

Assignment of support rights – the legal procedures by which a person receiving public assistance agrees to turn over to the state any right to child support, including arrearages, paid by the obligated parent in exchange for receipt of a cash assistance grant and other benefits. The money is used to defray the public assistance costs.

Child Support Enforcement (CSE) agency – agency that exists in the 54 states and territories and several Native American tribes, established by title IV-D (Four-D) of the Social Security Act, to locate noncustodial parents, establish paternity and establish and enforce child support orders.

Child Support Enforcement Program – the Federal/state/local partnership established under Part D of the Social Security Act to locate parents, establish paternity and child support orders and to enforce those orders.

Complaint – written document filed in court in which the person initiating the action names the persons, allegations, and relief sought.

Consent agreement – voluntary written admission of paternity or responsibility for support.

Consumer Credit Protection Act (CCPA) – Federal law that limits the amount that may be withheld from earnings.

Continuing Exclusive Jurisdiction (CEJ) – doctrine that only one support order can be in effect at any one time and that only one state has jurisdiction to modify the order.

Custodial parent – person with legal custody and with whom the child lives; may be a parent, other relative, legal guardian (JPS) or someone else.

Custody order – legal determination which establishes with whom a child shall live.

Default – failure of a defendant to appear, or file an answer or response in a civil case, after having been served with a summons and complaint.

Default judgment – decision made by the tribunal when the defendant fails to respond.

Defendant – person against whom a civil or criminal proceeding is begun.

Disestablishment – procedure by which a tribunal can nullify an order or a determination of paternity generally.

Disposable income – income remaining after subtracting mandatory deductions such as: Federal, state and local taxes; FICA and Medicare taxes; unemployment insurance, workers' compensation insurance; state employee retirement systems; additional deductions mandated by state law.

Electronic funds transfer (EFT) – transfer of money from one bank account to another or to a CSE agency.

Enforcement – obtaining payment of a child support or medical support obligation.

Establishment – the process of determining paternity and/or obtaining a child support order.

Family violence indicator – a notation in the case documents that information about a family's whereabouts cannot be released without a court order.

Federal Case Registry (FCR) – *A database that maintains all states' caseloads.*

Federal Income Tax Offset Program – a program under the Federal Office of Child Support Enforcement which makes available to state CSE Agencies a route for securing the tax refund of parents who have been certified as owing substantial amounts of child support.

Federal Parent Locator Service (FPLS) – a service operated by the Federal Office of Child Support Enforcement to help state CSE agencies locate parents in order to obtain child support payments; also used in cases of parental kidnapping related to custody and visitation determinations. The FPLS obtains address and employer information from Federal agencies.

Federally assisted Foster Care – a program, funded in part by the Federal government, under which a child is raised in a household by someone other than his or her own parent.

Financial Institution Data Match (FIDM) – a quarterly data match for the purpose of identifying accounts belonging to parents that owe past due child support.

Finding – a formal determination by a court, or administrative process, that has legal standing.

Full Faith and Credit – doctrine under which a state must honor an order or judgment entered in another state.

Garnishment – a legal proceeding under which part of a person's wages and/or assets is withheld for payment of a debt.

Genetic testing – analysis of inherited factors (usually by blood or tissue test) of mother, child, and alleged father which can help to prove or disprove that a particular man fathered a particular child.

Good cause – a reason for not trying to collect support from the father, usually because the father may be a threat to the mother and child(ren).

Guidelines – a standard method for setting child support obligations based on the income of the parent(s) and other factors as determined by state law.

IV-D (Four-D) Child Support Enforcement Program – the Federal/state/local and tribal child support programs established under title IV-D of the Social Security Act.

Immediate income withholding – automatic deductions from income which start as soon as the agreement for support is established (see income withholding).

Judgment – the official decision by the tribunal in authority on the rights and claims of the parties to an action.

Jurisdiction – legal authority which a court has over particular persons, certain types of cases, and in a defined geographical area.

Legal father – a man who is recognized by law as the male parent.

Lien – a claim upon property to prevent sale or transfer until a debt is satisfied.

Long arm statute – a law that permits one state to claim personal jurisdiction over someone who lives in another state.

Medicaid program – Federally funded medical support for low-income families.

Medical support – legal provision for payment of medical and dental bills.

National Directory of New Hires – a national repository of employment, unemployment insurance, and quarterly wage information.

Noncustodial parent – parent who does not have primary custody of a child.

Obligation – amount of money to be paid as support by the responsible parent and the manner by which it is to be paid.

Offset – amount of money taken from a parent's state or Federal income tax refund to satisfy a child support debt

Order – direction of a magistrate, judge or properly empowered administrative officer.

Parentage – the legal mother-child relationship and/or father-child relationship as determined by the state.

Paternity judgment – legal determination of fatherhood.

Plaintiff – person who brings an action, complains or sues in a civil case.

Presumption of paternity – a rule of law under which evidence of a man's paternity (e.g., voluntary acknowledgment, genetic test results) creates a presumption that the man is the father of a child. A rebuttable presumption can be overcome by evidence that the man is not the father, but it shifts the burden of proof to the father to disprove paternity.

Probability of paternity – the probability that the alleged father is the biological father of the child as indicated by genetic test results.

Pro se – when a party represents themselves in a legal matter.

PRWORA (Personal Responsibility and Work Opportunity Reconciliation Act) – legislation that was passed in 1996, which is also known as Welfare Reform.

Public assistance – money granted from the state/Federal government to a person or family for living expenses; eligibility is based on need.

State Parent Locator Service (SPLS) – a service operated by the state Child Support Enforcement Agencies to locate noncustodial parents to establish paternity, and establish and enforce child support obligations.

State Workforce Agencies (SWAs) – agencies that provide Quarterly Wage and Unemployment Insurance Compensation data to the NDNH.

Statute of limitations – the period during which someone can be held liable for an action or a debt; statutes of limitations for collecting child support vary from state to state.

Stay – an order by a court that suspends all or some of the proceedings in a case.

Temporary Assistance to Needy Families (TANF) – assistance payments made on behalf of children who don't have the financial support of one of their parents by reason of death, disability, or continued absence from the home. The program provides parents with job preparation, work and support services to help them become self-sufficient.

Tribal Organizations – organizations run by Native American tribes.

Tribunal – a court, administrative agency or quasi-judicial entity authorized to establish, enforce or modify support orders or to determine parentage.

Uniform Interstate Family Support Act (UIFSA), and *Uniform Reciprocal Enforcement of Support Act (URESA)* – laws enacted at the state level which provide mechanisms for establishing and enforcing support obligations when the noncustodial parent lives in one state and the custodial parent and the children live in another.

Visitation – the right of a noncustodial parent to visit or spend time with his or her children.

Voluntary acknowledgment of paternity – an acknowledgment by a man, or both parents, that the man is the father of a child, usually provided in writing on an affidavit or form.

Wage withholding – procedure by which automatic deductions are made from wages or income to pay some debt such as child support; may be voluntary or involuntary.

*****

For more information on how the child support system works in your state, contact your state Child Support Enforcement agency. For general information about the Child Support Enforcement Program, contact the Office of Child Support Enforcement, 370 L'Enfant Promenade, Washington, D.C. 20447, or visit the website at:
http://www.acf.hhs.gov/programs/cse

STATE CHILD SUPPORT ENFORCEMENT OFFICES

ALABAMA

Department of Human Resources
Child Support Enforcement Division
50 Ripley Street
Montgomery, AL 36130-1801
　　　　(334) 242-9300
　　　　(334) 242-0606 FAX
1-　　　800-284-4347

ALASKA

Child Support Services Division
Department of Revenue
550 West 7th Avenue, 2nd Floor
Suite 280
Anchorage, AK 99501-6699
　　　　1-800-478-3300
　　　　(907) 269-6813 FAX

ARIZONA

Division of Child Support Enforcement
Arizona Department of Economic Security
3443 N. Central, 4th Floor
Phoenix, AZ 85067
　　　　(602) 252-4045
　　　　(602) 274-8250 FAX

ARKANSAS

Office of Child Support Enforcement
Department of Finance and Administration
P.O. Box 8133
Little Rock, AR 72203-8133
Street Address:　400 E Capitol
　　　　　　Little Rock, AR 72203
　　　　(501) 682—6169
　　　　(501) 682-6002 FAX
1-　　　800-264-2445 (payments)
　　　1-800-247-4549 (program)

CALIFORNIA

Department of Child Support Services
P.O. Box 419064, Mail Station 10
Rancho Cordova, CA 95741-9064
(　　　866) 249-0773
　　　　(910) 464-5211 FAX

COLORADO

Division of Child Support Enforcement
Department of Human Services
1575 Sherman Street, 5th Floor
Denver, CO 80203-1714
(　　　303) 866-4300
　　　　(303) 866-4360 FAX

CONNECTICUT

Connecticut Department of Social Services
Bureau of Child Support Enforcement
25 Sigourney Street
Hartford, CT 06106-5033
(　　　860) 424-4989
　　　　(860) 951-2996 FAX
1-　　　888-233-7223
　　　　(information/payments)

DELAWARE

Division of Child Support Enforcement
Delaware Health and Social Services
P.O. Box 904
New Castle, DE 19720
(　　　302) 395-6500
　　　　(302) 577-7171 (customer
　　　　service)
　　　　(302) 395-6733 FAX

STATE CHILD SUPPORT ENFORCEMENT OFFICES

DISTRICT OF COLUMBIA

Child Support Services Division
Office of the Attorney General
Judiciary Square
441 Fourth Street, NW, 5th Floor
Washington, DC 20001
(202) 724-2131
        (202) 724-3710 FAX

FLORIDA

Child Support Enforcement
Department of Revenue
P.O. Box 8030
Tallahassee, FL 32399-7016
(8540) 922-9590
        (850) 921-0792 FAX
1-   800-622-5437

GEORGIA

Child Support Enforcement
Department of Human Resources
2 Peachtree Street, Suite 20460
Atlanta, GA 30303
(404) 657-3851
        (404) 657-3326 FAX

GUAM

Child Support Enforcement Division
The Justice Building
287 West O'Brien Drive
Hagatna, GU 96910
(671) 475-3324
        (671) 475-3203 FAX

HAWAII

Child Support Enforcement Agency
Office of Attorney general
601 Kamokila Boulevard, Suite 207
Kapolei, HI 96707
(808) 692-7000
        (808) 692-7134 FAX

IDAHO

Bureau of Child Support Services
Department of Health and Welfare
P.O. Box 83720
Boise, ID 83720-0036
1-   800-356-9868
        (208) 334-5571 FAX

ILLINOIS

Division of Child Support Enforcement
Illinois Department of Public Aid
509 South 6th Street, 6th Floor
Springfield, IL 62701
1-   800-447-4278
        (217) 524-4608 FAX
1-   877-225-7077 (payments)

INDIANA

Child Support Bureau
Division of Family and Children
402 W. Washington Street, Room W360
Indianapolis, IN 46204
(317) 233-5437
        (317) 233-4932 FAX

IOWA

Bureau of Collections
Department of Human Services
400 SW 8th Street, Suite M
Des Moines, IA 50319
(515) 281-5647
        (515) 281-8854 FAX
1-   888-229-9223

KANSAS

Child Support Enforcement Program
Department of Social and
 Rehabilitation Services
P.O. Box 497
Topeka, KS 66601
(785) 296-3237
        (785) 296-5206 FAX

Updated addresses/telephone
numbers: http://ocse.acf.hhs.gov/int/directories/index.cfm?fuseaction=main.extivdlist

STATE CHILD SUPPORT ENFORCEMENT OFFICES

KENTUCKY

Division of Child Support
Cabinet for Families and Children
P.O. Box 2150
Frankfort, KY 40602
Street Address: 730 Schenkel Lane
           Frankfort, KY 40602
(502) 564-2285
       (502) 564-5988 FAX
1-   800-248-1163

LOUISIANA

Office of Family Support
Support Enforcement Services
P.O. Box 94065
Baton Rouge, LA 70804
(225) 342-4780
       (225) 342-7397 FAX
1-   800-256-4650 (payments)

MAINE

Division of Support Enforcement
 and Recovery
Bureau of Family Independence
Department of Health and Human Services
268 Whitten Road – 11 State House Station
Augusta, ME 04333-0993
(207) 624-4100
       (207) 287-2334 FAX

MARYLAND

Child Support Enforcement Administration
Department of Human Resources
Saratoga State Center
311 West Saratoga Street, Room 301
Baltimore, MD 21201
(410) 767-7065
       (410) 333-6264 FAX
1-   800-332-6347

MASSACHUSETTS

Child Support Enforcement Division
Massachusetts Department of Revenue
P.O. Box 7057
Boston, MA 02204-7057
1-   800-332-2733
       (617) 887-7570 FAX

MICHIGAN

Office of Child Support
Department of Human Services
P.O. Box 30037
Lansing, MI 48909-7978
Street Address: 235 S. Grand Ave.
           Lansing, MI 48909
(517) 373-2035
       (517) 373-4980 FAX

MINNESOTA

Office of Child Support Enforcement
Department of Human Services
444 Lafayette Road, 4th Floor
St. Paul, MN 55155-3846
(651) 431-4400
       (651) 431-7517 FAX

MISSISSIPPI

Division of Child Support Enforcement
Department of Human Services
750 North State Street
Jackson, MS 39205
1-   800-434-5437
       (601) 359-4415 FAX
       1-800-354-6039 (Hines,
       Rankin and Madison
Counties)

Updated addresses/telephone
numbers: http://ocse.acf.hhs.gov/int/directories/index.cfm?fuseaction=main.extivdlist

STATE CHILD SUPPORT ENFORCEMENT OFFICES

MISSOURI

Division of Child Support Enforcement
Department of Social Services
P.O. Box 2320, 615 Howerton Court Bldg.
Jefferson City, MO 65101
1-   800-859-7999
         (573) 751-0507 FAX

MONTANA

Child Support
Department of Public and Human Services
3075 N. Montana Ave , Suite 112
Helena, MT 59620
         (406) 444-9855
         (406) 444-1370 FAX

NEBRASKA

Child Support Enforcement Office
Department of Health and Human Services
P.O. Box 220, South 17th Street
Lincoln, NE 68509-4728
(402) 471-1400
         (402) 471-7311 FAX
1-   877-631-9973

NEVADA

State of Nevada Division of Welfare
and Supportive Services
1470 College Parkway
Carson City, NV 89706-7942
(775) 684-0705
         (775) 684-0702 FAX
         (775) 684-7200 (customer
         Service)
         (702) 486-1646 (customer
         service)

NEW HAMPSHIRE

Division of Child Support Services
Department of Health and Human Services
129 Pleasant Street
Concord, NH 03301-8711
(603) 271-4427
         (603) 271-4787 FAX
1-   800-852-3345

NEW JERSEY

Office of Child Support
Department of Human Services
P.O. Box 716
Trenton, NJ 08625-0716
         (609) 588-2915
         (609) 588-2354 FAX
         1-877-655-4371 (automated
                    system)

NEW MEXICO

Child Support Enforcement Division
Department of Human Services
P.O. Box 25110
Santa Fe, NM 87502
Street Address: 2009 S. Pacheco
         Pollen Plaza
         Santa Fe, NM 87504
(505) 476-7207
         (505) 476-7045 FAX
1-   800-288-7207
1-   800-585-7631

NEW YORK

Division of Child Support Enforcement
Office of Temporary Assistance and
Disability
40 North Pearl Street, Room 13C
Albany, NY 12243-0001
(518) 474-9081
         (518) 486-3127 FAX
1-   888-208-4485

Updated addresses/telephone
numbers: http://ocse.acf.hhs.gov/int/directories/index.cfm?fuseaction=main.extivdlist

STATE CHILD SUPPORT ENFORCEMENT OFFICES

NORTH CAROLINA

Child Support Enforcement
Department of Human Resources
P.O. Box 20800
Raleigh, NC 27619-0800
(919) 225-3800
           (919) 212-3840 FAX
1-   800-992-9457

NORTH DAKOTA

Child Support Enforcement Agency
Department of Human Services
P.O. Box 7190
Bismarck, ND 58507-7190
(701) 328-3582
           (701) 328-5497 FAX
1-   800-231-4255

OHIO

Office of Child Support Enforcement
Department of Human Services and Jobs
 and Family Services
30 East Broad Street, 31st Floor
Columbus, OH 43215-3414
(614) 752-6561
           (614) 752-9760 FAX
1-   800-686-1556

OKLAHOMA

Child Support Enforcement Division
Department of Human Services
P.O. Box 53552
Oklahoma City, OK 73152
Street Address: 2409 N. Kelly Avenue
Annex   Building
           Oklahoma City, OK 73152
(405) 522-5871
           (405) 522-2753 FAX
1-   800-522-2922

OREGON

Division of Child Support
Oregon Department of Justice
494 State Street, SE, Suite 300
Salem, OR 97301
(503) 986-6166
           (503) 986-6158 FAX

PENNSYLVANIA

Bureau of Child Support Enforcement
Department of Public Welfare
P.O. Box 8018
Harrisburg, PA 17108-8018
1-   800-932-0211
           (717) 787-9706 FAX

PUERTO RICO

Department of the Family
P.O. Box 70376
San Juan, PR 00936-8376
Street Address: Majagua Street Bldg. 2
           Wing 4, 2nd Floor
           Rio Pedras, PR 00902-9938
(787) 767-1500
           (787) 723-6187 FAX

RHODE ISLAND

Office of Child Support Services
Department of Human Services
77 Dorrance Street
Providence, RI 02903
(401) 458-4400
           (401) 458-4407 FAX

STATE CHILD SUPPORT ENFORCEMENT OFFICES

SOUTH CAROLINA

Department of Social Services
Child Support Enforcement Division
P.O. Box 1469
Columbia, SC 29202-1469
(803) 898-9210
        (803) 898-9201 FAX
1-   800-768-5858
1-   800-768-6779 (payments)

SOUTH DAKOTA

Division of Child Support
Department of Social Services
700 Governor's Drive
Pierre, SD 57501-2291
(605) 773-3641
        (605) 773-5246 FAX
        1-800-286-9145 (Active Cases)

TENNESSEE

Child Support Services
Department of Human Services
400 Deadrick Street
Nashville, TN 37248-7400
(615) 313-4880
        (615) 532-2791 FAX
1-   800-838-6911

TEXAS

Child Support Division
Office of the Attorney General
P.O. Box 12017
Austin, TX 78741-2017
1-   800-252-8014
        (512) 460-6867 FAX

UTAH

Child Support Services
Office of Recovery Services
Department of Human Services
P.O. Box 45033
Salt Lake City, UT 84145-0033
(801) 536-8901
        (801) 536-8509 FAX
1-   800-257-9156

VERMONT

Office of Child Support
103 South Main Street
Waterbury, VT 05671-1901
1-   800-786-3214
        (802) 244-1483 FAX

VIRGIN ISLANDS

Child Support Enforcement
Department of Justice
Nisky Center, 2nd Floor, Suite 500
St. Thomas, VI 00802
(340) 777-3070
        (340) 775-3808 FAX
        (340) 799-3800 FAX (St. Croix)

VIRGINIA

Division of Child Support Enforcement
Department of Social Services
7 North Eight Street, 1st Floor
Richmond, VA 23219
1-   800-257-9986
1-   800-468-8894
        (804) 726-7476 FAX

STATE CHILD SUPPORT ENFORCEMENT OFFICES

WASHINGTON

Division of Child Support
Economic Services Administration
P.O. Box 9162
Olympia, WA 98507-9162
Street Address: 712 Pear Street, SE
        Olympia, WA 98507
(360) 664-664-5000
     (360) 664-5444 FAX
1-   800-457-6202

WEST VIRGINIA

Bureau of Child Support Enforcement
Department of Health and Human Resources
350 Capitol Street, Room 147
Charleston, WV 25301-3703
(304) 558-3780
     (304) 558-2445 FAX
1-   800-249-3778

WISCONSIN

Bureau of Child Support
Division of Economic Support
201 E. Washington, Room E200
P.O. Box 7935
Madison, WI 53707-7935
(608) 266-9909
     (608) 267-2824 FAX

WYOMING

Child Support Enforcement
Department of Family Services
122 W. 25th Herschler Bldg.
1301 1st Floor East
Cheyenne, WY 82002
(307) 777-6948
     (307) 777-5588 FAX

Updated addresses/telephone
numbers: http://ocse.acf.hhs.gov/int/directories/index.cfm?fuseaction=main.extivdlist

TRIBAL GRANTEE CONTACT INFORMATION

Central Council Tlingit & Haida
 Indian Tribes of Alaska
320 West Willoughby Ave., Suite 300
Juneau, AK 99801
P: 1 (800) 344-1432
F: (907) 463-7312

Cherokee Nation
Office of Child Support Enforcement
P.O. Box 557
Tahlequah, OK 74465-0557
P: (918) 453-5444
F: (918) 458-6165

Chickasaw Nation
Child Support Enforcement Dept.
P O Box 1809, 125 South Broadway
Ada, OK 74820
P: (580) 436-3419
F: (580) 436-3460

Confederated Tribes of the Umatilla
 Indian Reservation
Dept. Of Children & Family
 Services/CSE Office CTUIR
P.O. Box 638
Pendleton, OR 97801-0638
P: (541) 215-0852
F: (541-278-7462

Forest County Potawatomi Community
FCPC Tribal Child Support Agency
P.O. Box 340
5415 Everybody's Road
Crandon, WI 54520
P: (715) 478-7260
F: (715) 478-7331

Kaw Nation
Kaw Nation Child Support Services
P.O. Box 50
Kaw City, OK 74641
P: (580) 269-2003
F: (580) 269-2113

Keweenaw Bay Indian Community
Office of Child Support Services
16429 Bear Town Road
Baraga, MI 49908-9210
P: (906) 353-4566
F: (906) 353-8132

Lac du Flambeau Band of Lake
 Superior Chippewa Indians
LDF Tribal Child Support Agency
P.O. Box 1198
Lac du Flambeau, WI 54538
P: (715) 588-4236
F: (715) 588-9240

Lummi Nation
Lummi Nation Child Support Program
2616 Kwina Road
Bellingham, WA 98226
P: (360) 384-2326
F: (360) 312-9192

Menominee Indian Tribe of Wisconsin
Menominee Tribal Child Support
 Agency
P.O. Box 520
Keshena, WI 54135
P: (715) 799-5161
F: (715) 799-6061

For updated list of grantees and address/telephone numbers:
http://ocse.acf.hhs.gov/int/directories/index.cfm?fuseaction=main.tribalivd

TRIBAL GRANTEE CONTACT INFORMATION

Modoc Tribe of Oklahoma
P.O. Box 1110
21 N. Eight Tribes Trail
Miami, OK 74354
P: (918) 540-1501
F: (918) 540-1503

Muscogee (Creek) Nation
P.O. Box 580
Okmulgee, OK 74447
P: (918) 752-3181
F: (918) 756-2445

Navajo Nation
Dept. of Child Support Enforcement
P O Box 7050
Window Rock, AZ 86515
P: (928) 871-7195
F: (928) 871-7196

Nooksack Indian Tribe
P.O. Box 157
Deming, WA 98244
P: (360) 592-4158
F: (360) 592-5721

Oneida Tribe of Indians of
 Wisconsin
Oneida Nation Child Support Dept.
P.O. Box 365
Oneida, WI 54155
P: (920) 490-3766
F: (920) 490-3799

Osage Tribe of Oklahoma
Osage Nation Child Support Services
P.O. Box 1299, 255 Senior Dr.
Pawhuska, OK 74056
P: (918) 287-5575
F: (918) 287-5577

Penobscot Nation
Penobscot Nation Title IV-D Program
12 Wabanaki Way
Old Town, ME 04468
P: (207) 817-7328
F: (207) 827-9129

Ponca Tribe of Oklahoma
Ponca Nation Child Support
 Enforcement
Box 20, White Eagle Drive
Ponca City, OK 74601
P: (580) 765-2822
F: (580) 762-6868

Port Gamble S'Klallam Tribe
Child Support Program
31912 Little Boston Road, NE
Kingston, WA 98346
P: (360) 297-9668
F: (360) 297-9666

Puyallup Tribe of Indians
Child Support Enforcement
 Program
3009 East Portland Ave.
Tacoma, WA 98424
P: (253) 680-5744
F: (253) 896-1081

Quinault Indian Nation
Child Support Services
P.O. Box 189
Taholah, WA 98567
P: (360) 276-8211, ext 322
F: (360) 276-0008

For updated list of grantees and address/telephone numbers:
http://ocse.acf.hhs.gov/int/directories/index.cfm?fuseaction=main.tribalivd

TRIBAL GRANTEE CONTACT INFORMATION

Red Lake Band of Chippewa
Indians
Red Lake Nation Child Support
Program
P.O. Box 1020
Red Lake, MN 56671
P: (218) 679-2306
F: (218) 679-2390

Sisseton-Wahpeton Oyate Sioux Tribe
Office of Child Support Enforcement
P O Box 808
Agency Village, SD 57262
P: (605) 698-7131
F: (605) 698-7170

Three Affiliated Tribes
Division of Child Support Enforcement
Box 998
New Town, ND 58763
P: (701) 627-2860
F: (701) 627-3963

White Earth Nation
White Earth Nation Child Support
Program
P.O. Box 387
White Earth, MN 56591
P: (218) 983-3285, ext. 1324
F: (218) 983-3101

For updated list of grantees and address/telephone numbers:
http://ocse.acf hhs.gov/int/directories/index.cfm?fuseaction=main.tribalivd

REGIONAL OFFICES OF THE
OFFICE OF CHILD SUPPORT ENFORCEMENT

REGION I – CONNECTICUT, MAINE, MASSACHUSETTS, NEW HAMPSHIRE, RHODE ISLAND, VERMONT

OCSE Program Manager
Administration for Children and Families
John F. Kennedy Federal Building
Room   2000
Boston, MA 02203
(617)   565-2440

REGION II – NEW YORK, NEW JERSEY, PUERTO RICO, VIRGIN ISLANDS

OCSE Program Manager
Administration for Children and Families
Federal Building, Room 4114
26 Federal Plaza
New York, NY 10278
(212)   264-2890

REGION III – DELAWARE, MARYLAND, PENNSYLVANIA, VIRGINIA, WEST VIRGINIA, DISTRICT OF COLUMBIA

OCSE Program Manager
Administration for Children and Families
150 South Independence Mall West, Suite 864
Philadelphia, PA 19106-3499
(215)   861-4000

REGION IV – ALABAMA, FLORIDA, GEORGIA, KENTUCKY, MISSISSIPPI, NORTH CAROLINA, SOUTH CAROLINA, TENNESSEE

OCSE Program Manager
Administration for Children and Families
Federal   Center
61 Forsyth Street, SW, Suite 4M60
Atlanta, GA 30303-8909
(404)   562-2960

For updated address/telephone numbers:
http://ocse.acf hhs.gov/int/directories/index.cfm?fuseaction=main.extregofficemap

REGION V – ILLINOIS, INDIANA, MICHIGAN, MINNESOTA, OHIO, WISCONSIN

OCSE Program Manager
Administration for Children and Families
233 North Michigan Avenue, Suite 400
Chicago, IL 60601-5519
(312)   353-4863

REGION VI – ARKANSAS, LOUISIANA, NEW MEXICO, OKLAHOMA, TEXAS

OCSE Program Manager
Administration for Children and Families
1301 Young Street, Room 914 (ACF-3)
Dallas, TX 75202
(214)   767-9648

REGION VII – IOWA, KANSAS, MISSOURI, NEBRASKA

OCSE Program Manager
Administration for Children and Families
601 East 12th Street
Federal Building, Suite 276
Kansas City, MO 64106

REGION VIII – COLORADO, MONTANA, NORTH DAKOTA, SOUTH DAKOTA, UTAH, WYOMING

OCSE Program Manager
Administration for Children and Families
Federal Office Building
1961 Stout Street, 9th Floor
Denver, CO 80294-3538
(303)   844-1132

REGION IX – ARIZONA, CALIFORNIA, HAWAII, NEVADA, GUAM

OCSE Program Manager
Administration for Children and Families
90   7th Street, 9th Floor
San Francisco, CA 94103-6710
(415)   437-8400

For updated address/telephone numbers:
http://ocse.acf hhs.gov/int/directories/index.cfm?fuseaction=main.extregofficemap

REGION X – ALASKA, IDAHO, OREGON, WASHINGTON

OCSE Program Manager
Administration for Children and Families
2201 Sixth Avenue
Mail Stop RX-70
Seattle, WA 98121
(206)   615-2547

CHILD SUPPORT ENFORCEMENT RECORDS

Custodial Parent _____

Address _ _____

_____

Names of Dependent Children   Dates of Birth

_____   _____

_____ _   _____

_____ _   _____

_____ _   _____

Noncustodial Parent _____

Address(es) _____

_   _____

_   _____

Social Security Number   Date and Place of Birth

_____   _____

Employer(s) Dat   es

_____ _   _____

_____ _   _____

_____ _   _____

_____ _   _____

_____ _   _____

1

Child Support Enforcement Office

—   _____

—   _____

—   _____

Enforcement caseworker

—   _____

—   _____

Case Number   _____

State Enforcement Agency

—   _____

—   _____

—   _____

Lawyer   _____

—   _____

—   _____

Courts:

Custodial Parent   _____

—   _____

Noncustodial Parent   _____

_____

Present Support Obligation: $_____

To be paid   _____

CHILD SUPPORT ENFORCEMENT CASE LOG

Action Taken   Date   Outcome

NOTES

NOT   ES

For more information on how the child support system works in your state, contact your state Child Support Enforcement agency. For general information about the Child Support Enforcement Program, contact the Office of Child Support Enforcement, 370 L'Enfant Promenade, Aerospace Building, Washington, D.C. 20447, or visit the website at:
http://www.acf.hhs.gov/programs/cse